Praise fc

Pirtle's joy for life is clearly evident here, and it makes readers want to follow her advice.

RED CITY REVIEW

Every time I pick up this book it's a step forward on my path, it gives me the support I need.

Amazon Verified Review

I recommend this book for anyone who finds they need more hope for a brighter and lighter tomorrow.

Amazon Verified Review

JACQUELINE PIRTLE

365 Days of Happiness

Because happiness is a piece of cake!

A step-by-step guide to being happy

ISBN: 1732085102 ISBN-13: 978-1-7320851-0-7

Published by: Freaky Healer

Editor-in-chief: Bonnie Ramone
Editor: Zoe Pirtle
Editor/layout: Mitch Pirtle

Book cover design by Kingwood Creations kingwoodcreations.com

Author photo courtesy of Lionel Madiou madiouART.com

I want to let you know that ***365 Days of Happiness*** is a whole system, consisting of this bestseller ***365 Days of Happiness: Because happiness is a piece of cake*** (or the **Special Edition** with room for notes) and companion, the enlightening ***365 Days of Happiness*** journal workbook.

However, I made it so you can receive the benefit of learning how to live happily solely with reading a daily passage in this bestseller ***365 Days of Happiness: Because happiness is a piece of cake***, while also experiencing the full satisfaction by adding journaling through the terrific ***365 Days of Happiness*** journal workbook. Either way, I know you'll love my inspirational teachings.

Also, the book ***365 Days of Happiness: Because happiness is a piece of cake*** is available as a companion mobile application, for both Android and iPhone. You can find out more at www.freakyhealer.com

So before you dive in, I want to thank you for hopping on the happiness train with me! I truly hope you enjoy ***365 Days of Happiness*** as much as I loved writing it, and if you do, it would be wonderful if you could take a short minute and leave a review on Amazon.com and Goodreads.com as soon as you can. Your kind feedback helps other readers find my books easier, and be happy faster. Consider it a happy deed for the world.

Thank you!

From the bottom of my heart...

I could not have finished this book without the help of insanely talented and dedicated professionals.

I want to thank Bonnie Ramone for her editorial mastery; Zoe Pirtle for her editorial attention to detail skills; Mitch Pirtle for his all-round support and layout love; kingwoodcreations.com for their fun and polished book cover design; and madiouART.com for an amazing photo shoot.

A huge "Thank You!" to everyone and everything that supported me and urged me to write *365 Days of Happiness: Because happiness is a piece of cake*.

You are all my heroes!

Imagine that you are a bee, living your new day, jumping from happiness to happiness. Every jump you take, some happiness sticks on your being; like pollen on the bee. It adds up, resulting in you getting happier and happier.

Now imagine that as this happy bee you also journal about your happy bee-life—making happiness stick better, so much so that other bees are wondering how.

That is what reading and journaling in the 365 Days of Happiness Series will do for you.

So what are you waiting for?

Go happy-ing, go buzzing!

I dedicate ***365 Days of Happiness: Because happiness is a piece of cake*** to my wonderful husband Mitch Pirtle, my amazing kids Zoe Pirtle and Till Pirtle, and our sweet cats. I could not have written this book without your support, love, laughter, smiles and cheerleading efforts.

Thank you!

I love you all to the moon and back.

Dear reader,

I am absolutely thrilled that you got your hands on this book and are entertaining the wish to learn how to BE happy and live happily ever after!

You might think it's hard or even impossible to be happy every single day. Let me tell you this: It is not. No matter what is happening, you can always shift from being un-happy to BE and live your own happiness. Promise. I have tested this statement through all the ups and downs throughout my life as a woman, wife, mom, energy healer, mindfulness guide, and teacher of life.

But why even BE and live happy?

By BE I mean your whole YOU (body, mind, soul, and consciousness) being happy, and by live, I mean you experiencing this physical life as happy.

1. For starters, a happy life is a fun and fulfilled experience. A happy being has a healthy physical body, a mind producing joyous thoughts, a soul easy to connect to, and a vivid conscious! ness to experience life through. When I am happy, my health picks up, I know exactly what I need and want, everything goes right for me, and I experience my life as magical. I call this state my high-for-life frequency.

2. No pressure, but I see it as everyone's responsibility to BE their best happy them! I base this on the fact that nothing is ever separate, everything IS always ONE, and that we are all made of energy; we are all connected, and we share our energies at all times. You make the world a better place when you are happy!

3. I BELIEVE our truth in this physical life is to BE and live happily, and I KNOW that everyone deserves to learn how to achieve that.

And what is it all about?

Unleash the power of your body, mind, soul, and consciousness to acknowledge all there IS for you. To get a deeper understanding of yourself, everything, and everyone beyond your physical limitations. Dive happily and vividly into the adventure of your life.

So how does it work?

Happiness is a live moment-to-moment kind of feeling. It is an exercise in mindfulness that shows up in many different ways. There is no right or wrong, no imperfect or perfect, and no good or bad time. Happiness is born when you choose it, commit to it, and when you want to learn how to BE it.

I decided to spend every day of 2017 devoted to my own happiness. I wrote every single day about the things I do to honor my own joy, and I used these writings to create this 365 day step-by-step guide, so I could teach you how to shift to BE and live in a high-for-life frequency of happiness too, no matter where you are in your life right now. I started writing these for myself, but I have a little sneaky intent to touch your heart every day and initiate new learning, understanding, knowledge, and wisdom for you to get closer to your true authentic self.

Some of the guidance you may choose to practice only on that given day, and others you will fall in love with and adopt to continue for the rest of your life. Either way, I hope they will all be rooted in your being, and that your created happiness stays with you for your whole life and beyond.

So place this book next to your bed and let it be the first inspiration nourishing your body, mind, soul, and consciousness in the morning. Drenching your new day in a high-for-life energy, which you then can feel, think, smell, taste, hear, and see all day long.

Yes, you read this right. I believe very strongly that until you taste your day, you are not living as vividly as you could be, so let me share with you.

Creating this book changed me immensely and I hope it does the same for you.

With the happiest wishes for you,
    Jacqueline Pirtle

Day 1

Amazing things will happen when you start a love affair with your own happiness!

And I mean, to really be smitten with your happiness until you can't take your thoughts off it anymore. All it takes is a first date, and then a commitment.

Consciously plan a wonderful time for yourself. It can be as simple as sitting by a window with a cup of hot tea. Invite your happiness into your life with saying "I am ready to BE and live happy." Feel your heart filling with excitement. Then make a commitment to give your happiness your undivided attention and love.

Start when you open your eyes in the morning, "Good glorious morning my dear Happiness, how are you today, and what magnificent joy are we going to create?" *Listen, because happiness replies to you every time.* And then start your day with the plans you made together.

Check-in at noon, "Hi my dear Happiness, how are we doing? Lost each other there for a moment when I got frustrated, but found each other again. Awesome. What delight are we creating for the afternoon?" *Listen, because happiness always answers.*

The next check-in is in the evening, "Welcome home Happiness, let's relax and enjoy each other!"

The last conversation of the day is before you fall asleep, "My beautiful Happiness, I love you and I am the most blessed being in the world to have you by my side. Life is amazing with you."

That IS happiness!

Day 2

Everything and everyone together make up this magnificent ocean of vibrating energy that is our beautiful universe!

- Everything is the same vibrating energy.
- Everything vibrates in different frequencies.
- Everything is connected, ONE—is sharing energy
- Everything can shift to BE and live in different frequencies.

You and me, no matter where we are, we are both energy, vibrating in certain frequencies and connected through our energies. Which means a rock and tree, train and car, insect and butterfly, boring book, beautiful song, tough situation, mean and nice people, and animals are all energy too; vibrating in certain frequencies and connected with you and me through our energies. They too make up this beautiful universe, just like you and me.

Every thought, emotion, action, and word is energy, vibrating in certain frequencies and connected with you and me. And since nothing is ever separate, but actually always connected, the effect of all we do, say, see, hear, taste, smell, think, and feel is always spread and shared with everything and everyone in our beautiful universe and beyond.

In your new day, be aware of that *connectedness, same-ness,* and *one-ness.* Do, say, see, hear, taste, smell, feel, and think with the understanding that all of you effects all of everyone and everything.

That IS happiness!

Day 3

The best cookie recipe makes delicious and enjoyable cookies! The best happiness recipe makes a delicious and enjoyable life!

- Acknowledge everything and everyone without judgment.
- Accept everything and everyone.
- Respect everything and everyone.
- Appreciate everything and everyone.
- Thank everything and everyone.
- Love everything and everyone.

With everything and everyone, I mean all, without exceptions! Because everything and everyone is in your life for a reason.

Acknowledging all in this way, releases resistance; and without your resistance you can shift smoothly with all that is happening for you. Who knows, you might even love it!

Life is an ever changing and constant moving experience: it is naturally so. Every split second is new, different, and fresh. That means every split second you get new opportunities and chances for a change to happen.

Use those split seconds, and make your delicious and enjoyable new day!

That IS happiness!

Day 4

Imagine you are waking up to these exciting words:

"Good morning beautiful being! I am happy you opened your eyes today. Get ready and come, because we have someone gorgeous waiting impatiently for you."

You ask "Who is it?"

"It is your delicious new given day! And it has a magnificent question for you. So come!"

You rush out of bed, get ready with speed and fly down the stairs into the living room. There it is, your incredible new day! You smile with excitement and say "Hello!"

Your new day smiles back and asks with enthusiasm, "May I have this dance today?" It charmingly offers you its hand and time, in the hopes you will go dance and create magic together. All day long.

What are you going to do?

Please tell me you accept that invitation with excitement and gratitude, and go dance to whatever music comes your way today.

Please tell me you will flow graciously in those dance moves with your new day, smiling and laughing with every move, creating magic together—All day long!

I think I hear you say "Yes!"

Fantastic!

That IS happiness!

Day 5

Personalize the "when" and the "what" that shifts you to BE and live in your own high-for-life frequency! Because getting personal with it creates clarity, understanding, knowledge, and wisdom about yourself.

So *what* makes you feel like you could hug the whole world? And *when* do you feel like you could hug the whole world?

- Listening or dancing to music?
- Exercising or playing sports?
- Meditating or walking in nature?
- A cup of tea or a piece of cake?

Become aware of the "when" and the "what", then make a list of all these high-for-life ingredients. Make it a priority to schedule them throughout your new day. If you happen to catch yourself feeling anything less than wonderful look at your list, and pick any of your ingredients that are possible to practice right then so you can shift back.

Have fun creating your personal happiness list!

That IS happiness!

Day 6

Imagine a bird! Free to fly whenever it wants, and wherever it wants.

You are as free as that bird!

- Because you are free to choose and think.
- You are free to do, say and hear.
- You are free to feel or not feel.
- You are free to taste and smell.
- You are free to play and smile.
- You are free to be happy or un-happy, healthy or unhealthy.
- You are free to be kind and to serve, or not kind and not to serve.
- You are free of your past, free to be in your now, and free for your future.

Knowing that, close your eyes and say out loud "I am free!" Feel yourself flying!

Now go and live your absolute freedom, and let it take you to your heart's desires in your new day.

That IS happiness!

Day 7

Imagine a person laughing so hard that tears are rolling down their cheeks. And even if they tried, they can't stop laughing. Now notice everyone and everything around them, and how they start to laugh too. By now, all you see is laughter.

See, hear, taste, smell, think, and feel how everyone and everything around that laughing person shifts to a happy frequency.

Laughing carries an energy of joy, silliness, playfulness, happiness, and fun. When you laugh, you immediately shift to BE and live in a high-for-life frequency. And with that, you shift everything and everyone around you too. Because everything is energy, connected with each other, and shares their energy.

Now let's say you are not laughing, but you make someone else laugh. Them laughing automatically shifts them to BE and live in that fun frequency, and they pull you with them, given you are open and receiving.

If you choose to make laughing your default reaction, no matter what is happening for you, you will experience everything and everyone through your laughing filter. And from there your reactions will be with humor.

So go, be a *professional laugher* in your new day!

That IS happiness!

Day 8

Wish lists are magical, they come with the energy of desires, wishes, hope, happiness, gifts, dreams, and feel-good intentions.

Wish lists for exceptional self-care are even more powerful, because they carry the added energy of self-love, self-compassion, self-acceptance, self-respect, self-appreciation, and self-gratitude.

So let's create that amazing wish-list for your exceptional self-care:

- I wish for me to treat myself like my own best friend.
- I wish for me to be loving, gentle, and understanding towards myself.
- I wish for me to do whatever it takes to feel amazing.
- I wish for me to eat fitting food, drink plenty of water, exercise, and breathe deep.
- I wish for me to relax and spend time in quiet and peace.

Make your self-care wish list fitting for you and act on your wishes often in your new day!

If at some point you find your list to be out-dated, don't worry, it means you outgrew it. You are moving forward in your life. Which is fantastic! Simply update it accordingly.

That IS happiness!

Day 9

You matter!!!

You are an important part of this physical life and time. Without you, a lot of things and happenings would not be. They would be missing, and make this physical life and time incomplete.

But there is more... Everything you do and are matters because everything is energy, connected, and shares their energy. So you being happy and feeling good matters infinitely, because you share your happiness with everything and everyone.

You are important and your impact on everything and everyone is huge.

So let me tell you that:

- Your body, mind, soul, and consciousness matter!
- Your love and light matters!
- Your happiness and you feeling good matters!
- Your thoughts, actions, and words matter!
- Your smile and your kindness matters!

In this new day of yours, realize how much you matter. And then go, live your new day, choosing to matter by being happy and feeling good.

Because if you are happy, an important part of the world is happy.

That IS happiness!

Day 10

Imagine you are holding a bug catcher net in your hands, but instead of catching insects, you are catching smiles.

Yes! You are a smile catcher!

Smiles naturally carry the energy of joy, happiness, fun, playfulness, and love. Smiling and receiving a smile shifts you to BE and live in that high-for-life frequency.

So...

- How many smiles can you give to everything and everyone around you in your new day?
- How many smiles can you receive in return?
- How many smiles are you gifted by others... without making a smile effort on your part?

Everyone and everything involved in those smiles will experience their new day in a state of happiness. And that splendid energy will spread wider and wider.

Be the best *smile catcher* ever!

That IS happiness!

Day 11

Imagination is your most personal and powerful happiness creator, because there are no limits. You can always imagine as much cheer as you wish to experience. And you have access to it 24 hours a day—which means you can imagine as much happiness as you like, and it is free!

So lets infuse what comes into your awareness with your imagination and create your own joy all day long:

Let's say you are out and about and notice a flower. Right there is your opportunity to create delight by imagining you are a beautiful butterfly in a magnificent garden, and you get to sit and sunbathe on this flower. *Feel this splendidness!*

Maybe you see a bird. Imagine you are jumping on its back, and go flying to wherever you like. *Feel this adventure!*

When you get yourself ready for your new day, imagine you are a king or queen; getting ready for a noble day. *Feel this highness!*

Or when you watch the trash guys remove your trash, imagine they just took all your toxic and un-fitting feelings and thoughts with them. *Feel the lightness!*

These are only a few imagination possibilities. Take what is in your awareness and imagine what feeds your heart. Play around, get all crazy with it, and feel how everything turns into your personal happiness playground.

That IS happiness!

Day 12

Imagine the most beautiful and magical palace ever. It is built strong and secure, and it comes with a powerful and sacred energy. It is taken care of with excellence, admired and celebrated with grace. A truly magical place, filled with miracles. And you get to live there!

That magical palace is your physical body, hosting your mind, soul, and consciousness!

Your physical body is built strong and secure, and it comes with a powerful and sacred energy. It wants you to take excellent care of it, admire it and celebrate it, with grace. It is a truly magical place, filled with miracles just like that magical palace you imagined.

And it has a voice that wants to be heard!

It constantly communicates its needs with you. Tired means it needs rest or sleep *now*. Hungry means it needs nutrition *now*. Pain means it needs attention *now*. Anger means it needs a reset *now*. Sadness means it needs nurturing *now*. And the NOW is super important, because your physical body tells you that very clearly.

In your new day, pay attention and hear, taste, smell, feel, see, and think of your magical palace often. Give it what it is asking for... or even better, give it what it has not yet asked for.

Accept, respect, appreciate, thank, and love your physical body so it can be and live its truth, as a magical palace filled with miracles, for you.

That IS happiness!

Day 13

When you check in with yourself, you gain knowledge, understanding, and wisdom!

So ask yourself right now:

- How AM I right now?
- How AM I with being here right now?
- How AM I with breathing right now?
- How AM I experiencing what is happening for me right now?

Acknowledge the clarity in the answers you receive, without getting emotionally entangled or judging. Accept, respect, appreciate, thank, and love them for the knowledge, understanding, and wisdom they bring.

If you got a feel-good answer, stay feeling good with indulging in this high-for-life frequency. Keep doing what you are doing because it is working. And with that, create more of your happiness.

If you did *not* get a feel-good answer, ask yourself how you can make your now better. For example, if a superior feeling can be created by indulging in a piece of chocolate, go enjoy that chocolate and feel your shift to BE and live in a happier frequency. If you can create it by rest, go rest and feel your shift to a more desirable feeling. Do whatever it takes!

In your new day, check in often and act on it. Little-by-little, you get to know yourself deeper, and can feel better and better.

That IS happiness!

Day 14

Imagine you are writing a good old-fashioned love letter. You pick a nice sheet of paper and make sure your pen is writing evenly. Then, think about how you feel and what you want to say. You smile and start writing your beautiful love words. While you write, you feel amazing and in so much love.

Now visualize the recipient receiving, opening, and reading your love letter. See that person smile and fill up with all your love and happiness you put in the creation of that letter.

That love was created in you, put on that paper, and then received by the recipient. It was shared and spread because everything is energy, connected, and shares their energy. In the case of that letter, the writer is energy, the feelings and thoughts of the writer are energy, the paper and ink are energy, the words are energy, the reader is energy, and the reader's feelings and thoughts are energy.

At the end you feel amazing and create amazing energy, and the reader feels amazing and creates amazing energy. Which shifts both of you to BE and live in a wonderful high-for-life frequency. And that goodness is spread to everything and everyone.

All that... with your love letter!

You will create the same beautiful energy with little love and happiness notes, texts, emails, and voice messages for others.

In your new day, be this messenger of love for others.

That IS happiness!

Day 15

Be clear with *how* you are, when in your personal high-for-life frequency!

Ask yourself the following questions and visualize your answers:

- How do I feel in my high-for-life frequency?
- How do I see everything in my pleased frequency?
- How do I hear, taste, and smell everything in my joyous frequency?
- How do I think in my cheerful frequency?
- How much do I love myself in my delighted frequency?
- How happy am I in my radiant frequency?
- How much do I enjoy my life in my high-for-life frequency?

I promise you that you will witness a picture of your best feeling version of YOU!

In your new day, visualize your answers often. It will bring clarity and shift you to BE and live in your personal feel-good frequency, which you will share with everyone and everything around you.

You might even start a high-for-life movement by practicing this!

That IS happiness!

Day 16

Imagine waking up, smiling, and saying, "This is already and will be the best day ever!"

When this is the first thing you say when you open your eyes, you set an amazing tone and intention for your new day, because that sentence carries an energy of *great-ness*, magnificence, power, and that everything is possible. It also shifts you to BE and live in a frequency of excitement to live your fabulous new day. And you create an infinite amount of positive energy with saying it... which means you are ready for your new best day ever!

You will go out there touching everything and everyone with your high-for-life energy, inspiring them to shift too. And all that goodness returns back to you like a boomerang because everything is energy, connected, and shares their energy.

Take it even further and continue saying it during your day, to keep that fabulous tone and intention flowing all day long.

You are an energy-changer for the world! Be and live that power!

That IS happiness!

Day 17

Are you happy right now?

Such a simple, yet incredibly important and valuable question.

Asking yourself "Am I happy right now?" will give you immediate understanding and clarity as to how you are doing in the feeling department.

- If your answer is yes, keep rocking your happiness. It suits you!
- If your answer is anything less than yes, grab this moment and do whatever it takes to shift yourself to any kind of happiness.

Consciously expressing gratitude, focusing on seeing all beauty, smelling deliciousness, tasting *yumminess*, hearing wonderful sounds, and feeling the magic in and around you works wonders.

And by all means, if you need to, take all support available. For me, chocolate always does the shift.

Also, ask others "Are you happy?" This amazing question has the same effect on them! Which means you give them an opportunity to either consciously feel their happiness, or shift to their happiness if they are not there.

Ask away in your new day, and with that, remind yourself and others to be happy!

That IS happiness!

Day 18

Imagine your own perfect high-for-life walking path. It can be big or small, through a meadow, a city, a forest, or at the beach. Make it fitting for you.

Now soak your path with different feel-good energies you desire: happy, playful, healthy, loving, peaceful, active, relaxed, or adventurous.

When finished, see, hear, taste, smell, think, and feel yourself entering your path. Start walking it. If you must, skip or run on it. Smile! Feel how you shift to BE and live in the high-for-life frequency of the wonderful path you created for yourself!

That path is the path you want to walk on while experiencing your new day. And now that you know how good it feels when you walk on your perfect path, you want to commit to stay on it all day long.

If you happen to wander off, simply re-visualize it. See yourself going back on it. Feel how good it feels there, and start walking it again. You will know if you have wandered off, because you will start feeling, seeing, hearing, tasting, smelling, and thinking anything less than what you created your path with earlier in your day.

You are now a high-for-life path owner. Keep it clean and happy!

That IS happiness!

Day 19

Feel, feel, and feel some more!

Ask yourself about everything that catches your awareness, "How or what do I feel while seeing, hearing, smelling, tasting, feeling, or thinking about this?"

Fully feel the first feeling that comes to your mind, even if it is anger or sadness. Feel it for as long as it feels good, and then move to the next feeling opportunity. For example: if you are angry, feel your anger. And once your anger does not feel good anymore, move on to the next awareness-catching happening.

Important is to never stay long and grow roots in a feeling that does not feel good, because it fills every cell of your body, mind, soul, and consciousness with unhealthy energy.

If you ask but don't feel anything, have no worries. Simply move on to the next awareness-catching opportunity coming your way.

Practicing on feeling your emotions trains your feeling muscles. And we all know a trained muscle is strong, powerful, and healthy.

The more you feel, the better you get to know yourself, and the more comfortable you will be with what and how you feel. So feel and feel some more in your new day!

That IS happiness!

Day 20

Imagine you do the same things at the same time every single day!

You eat at the same time, the same food every single day. You get dressed at the same time, wearing the same clothing every day. You live the same way every single day.

Do you think your experience of life is the fullest it can possibly be? No!

So shake things up in your new day:

- Instead of coffee have tea.
- Instead of a sandwich at the usual cafe, have a salad at a new eatery.
- Instead of your usual route, take a new route.
- Instead of wearing your usual clothing, wear something different.
- Instead of cleaning your house from front to back, start at the back going to the front.

Shaking up your routine will give you new experiences, and with that, you will shift the way you see, feel, smell, taste, think, and hear what is happening for you. Shaking things up also creates new opportunities for you that do not exist in your old ways of living.

A shaken-up life is filled with new spontaneous wonders!

That IS happiness!

Day 21

Follow your heart! It always knows!

Asking your heart produces unquestionable clarity of what you really want and love. It nourishes your passion to feel good and be truthful to yourself. It enriches your being as a person, partner, parent, friend, boss, and light-love creator. You shift to BE and live in your heart with asking.

Once you heard your heart answer, don't over-think. Just do as it says because it is always right!

The way to discern if the answer is coming from your heart or head is to FEEL. Answers from your heart FEEL good and you can feel your body, mind, soul, and consciousness jumping with joy. Answers from your mind, however, are not of the *touchy-feely* nature; they simply THINK good.

Every time you ask your heart or get back to your heart's truth, you erase your old un-fitting ways bit by bit and record new, fitting ways that you choose to be your truth.

If you ever catch yourself saying or thinking to yourself "Just give up!" (or something of that sort), give it your best smile and say or think "No!" Get back on track by asking your heart what it wants. And then just do it!

Always ask - but never question - your heart!

That IS happiness!

Day 22

Watch out, inspirations are about to get you... if you let them!

Start your new day by setting the intention to be open, and receive all inspirations coming your way!

Be inspired from within, by all inspirations you receive from your inner source. Hear a little voice—listen to it. See a little vision—believe it. Feel a little magic—live it. Go ahead, follow them all!

Be inspired by all that is around you, in your awareness. By the food and drinks you are gifted to enjoy, by kids, nature, and people. By colors, words, sounds, and smells. Feel, think, hear, taste, smell, and see it all!

All inspirations are sparks to enrich your life, and they bring you clarity on either how you want it... or how you don't want it.

Be inspired, and be an *inspirer*!

That IS happiness!

Day 23

We live in a universe where everything is made of energy and vibrates in different frequencies.

The energy of love vibrates in a high frequency, whereas the energy of anger vibrates in a lower frequency. Optimally, you want to be in a frequency of high vibrations, because that is where you feel good.

When lower energies pop up, you shift your energy to vibrate in a lower frequency. No harm done, they are all a normal part in all of us. Simply acknowledge them and accept, respect, appreciate, thank, and love them for being part of you. Then, without growing roots there, shift yourself back to energies that vibrate in a higher feel good frequency as soon as possible.

For example: You are angry. Acknowledge your anger without minding the why. Honor it with saying, "I accept you as part of me. I respect you as a powerful force in me. I appreciate you for the fuel you are for me. I thank you for the clarity you bring. I love you as my warrior energy." This will release any resistance you have towards your anger and shifts you to BE and live in a frequency of being in peace with your anger.

Practicing this pulls all the energies of you—high and low—together into one magical being, that is honored, celebrated, and loved as a whole.

That IS happiness!

Day 24

Miracles are like cakes!

- Someone has to have the desire and be open to baking a cake.
- Someone has to have the facility to make it.
- Someone has to have a recipe for the cake.
- Someone has to have the willingness to get all the ingredients.
- Someone has to actually bake it.
- Someone has to be open to receiving and eating the cake.

Without all these someones, there would not be a cake; at least not in a manifested way. It might simply stay a desire or a wish. Miracles are no different!

- *Someone* has to have the desire and be open to a miracle. So ask for a miracle!
- *Someone* has to have the facility to form a miracle. You as a whole are that facility!
- *Someone* has to have a recipe to make a miracle possible. You being happy is the recipe!
- *Someone* has to have the willingness to get all the ingredients together. Every happy moment is one of those ingredients.
- *Someone* has to actually make the miracle. That is not your job, the universe will do that for you.
- *Someone* has to be open to receive and accept the miracle. That would be you, so be open, ready, and receiving!

Without all these *someones*, there would not be a miracle; at least not in a manifested way. It would simply stay a desire or a wish.

You are a conduit for miracles. Without your presence there would not be miracles, and without being open and receiving miracles cannot form for you.

So be that someone! Be a miracle worker!

That IS happiness!

Day 25

Imagine that you are running or speed walking in nature. You are happy to be moving so fast and energetic. But then you see a colorful bird. Decisions, decisions...

If you keep running or speed walking, you would get to your finish line fast and on time, but you will not be able to watch the bird. If you slow down for a bit, you get to watch this colorful bird, but will get to your finish line slower and not on time.

Option 1 will make sure the focus is on your goal, but it does not really nourish you with the experiences that are available for you while you make your way though the world—which means you are not receiving spontaneously and are not creating as vividly as you could.

Option 2 delays the goal but nourishes your being on the way, with all that is there for you to experience. You receive spontaneous opportunities and create vividly as you go.

Now you might say that you cannot always slow down or delay all your goals. *And that is a fair thought.*

But even if you can only slow down and delay your goal for one minute per hour while you are awake, that means you slowed down about 16 minutes in your new day. And in 16 minutes you can easily watch that colorful bird, spontaneously flying into your awareness to co-create magic with you.

Slowing down means you create and experience unplanned magic!

That IS happiness!

Day 26

Make your energetic space wide, and root deep!

Creating and maintaining your own wide energetic space (where your light and being can shine!) is essential for your happiness. So is grounding your energetic being with strong deep roots that nourish and preserve your bright light.

Here is a powerful practice to "space wide and root deep:"

Close your eyes and focus on your deep breathing. Fall in love with your beautiful breath. Smile!

Imagine that with every breath in, you expand your light and energetic space wide and big. Feel your energetic being growing boundless.

Then, visualize that with every breath out, you ground and root your light and being down through the bottom of your feet, deep into Mother Earth. Feel your energetic roots grow deep and strong.

Repeat this as long as you would like.

Notice the rhythm and harmony in this dance between widening your light and deepening your roots, and feel your shift to BE and live in a wide and deep frequency.

In your new day, play with this a few minutes here and there. It also works with your eyes wide open, while hustling and bustling in your amazing business of life.

That IS happiness!

Day 27

Imagine you are waking up, and all you can think of is "I love everything!"

- I love my new day.
- I love every breath that I take.
- I love my physical body, mind, soul, and consciousness.
- I love all clothing I wear in my new day.
- I love all the magic and miracles that are waiting for me.
- I love all the food and drink that goes into my body.
- I love the ground beneath every step I take.
- I love all the sounds around me.
- I love everyone and everything showing up in my new day.
- I love my laughter, smile, and voice.
- And... I love all the non-fitting happenings in my life, all that annoys me, and all contrasts that are for me.

You simply commit to love it all in your new day.

Practicing to love everything and everyone shifts you to BE and live in a high-for-life frequency of love, which means your new day and every experience in it, will be based on your love.

This might just be the most love-filled day you have ever had!

That IS happiness!

Day 28

Kindness is a necessity for happiness and health!

Every split second of your new day presents millions of opportunities to be and show kindness towards yourself and others, which means you get unlimited chances to be happy and healthy and shift others to be happy and healthy too.

Here is what kindness initiates:

- Kindness opens hearts!
- Kindness enlightens!
- Kindness initiates mindfulness!
- Kindness heals!
- Kindness creates happiness!
- Kindness spreads magic!
- Kindness creates love!

Making the focus of your new day all about kindness shifts you to BE and live in a high-for-life frequency, which you will share with everything and everyone, spreading it wider and wider.

Also notice all kindness around you: in peoples' actions and faces, in nature, situations, and where the word "kindness" is written. Feel that kindness, and enjoy your shift to happiness and health.

That IS happiness!

Day 29

Imagine you are looking at a baby, human or animal. You immediately go "Aww, how precious!" You feel, hear, taste, smell, think, and see the gentleness, perfectness, and love in this experience.

In this scenario, life and nature show you how beautiful, perfect, gentle, and loving life is.

You ARE life!
You ARE nature!

This means you are that gentleness, perfectness, and love too.

Take moments in your new day where you focus on your gentle, perfect, and loving side. Feel it in your smile and in your eyes. Hear it in your voice. See it in your actions, movements, and your resting time. And notice it in your enjoying of life.

Become aware of the gentleness, perfectness, and love in everything and everyone around you. And enjoy the shift to BE and live in your high-for-life frequency which brings you directly into your heart, because that is where all this goodness lives.

This makes for a gentle, perfect and loving day!

That IS happiness!

Day 30

Be conscious about all your forward steps you will take in your new day!

The word "step" and the activity of taking a step carry the energy of movement, change, shifting, and aliveness. And the word "forward" with the action of moving forward carry the energy of ahead, next, onward, advancing, and progress.

So when you take a forward step and you are mindful about that advancing action, you shift to BE and live in a forward-moving high-for-life frequency. And that powerful energy will be sent to every single cell of your body, mind, soul, and consciousness. A thriving energy to be filled with.

Use every forward step you take in your new day to enjoy a forward way of being!

That IS happiness!

Day 31

Imagine standing on the top of a mountain with both of your arms stretched high up in the air. You close your eyes, you breathe deep, and think (or say or shout!) "I AM alive!" Feel this!

These powerful words carry the energy of celebration, gratefulness, appreciation, aliveness, adventures, and possibilities. Saying or thinking them shifts you to BE and live in that high-for-life frequency.

They also initiate a deep appreciation for waking up today, for breathing, and for receiving the gift of experiencing life right now.

And they create a feeling of being free, limitless, and infinitely powerful.

"I AM alive!" means you can go out there today, live with power, and create whatever you desire; because you are vibrantly and fully alive. It means you can smell your food, taste the water you drink, see your loved ones, hear the music, feel the energy, and think about everything vividly.

"I AM alive!" means you can be as happy as you wish to be, and you can enjoy life with every cell of your amazing body, mind, soul, and consciousness, as much as you like.

Go be alive!

That IS happiness!

Day 32

The most powerful and stable place for you to BE and live in is your heart.

It's also where the most powerful and stable energy for you to live through is created—your love!

Being in your heart means you are aligned with who you really are. You are grounded and strong, you have clarity about what you need and want, you are deeply connected with your self-love, and nothing or nobody can shift you to feel anything less than good. There, you are at your most powerful. You live in your truth and through your love.

There is really no grander high-for-life place to be.

So, go move all your belongings into your heart, sign a lease for life, and take exceptional care of your stable and powerful place called home. You won't regret it!

That IS happiness!

Day 33

Imagine you are the proud owner of a small spa hotel, taking great pride in giving your guests an amazing experience while staying at your magnificent place.

One of your spectacular and loved services is that you check in with your guests often, to see how they feel, ask what they desire, and how you can serve them. It makes you feel amazing, and your guests feel special, loved, taken care of, and pampered. Taking little spa check-ins for yourself during your new day has the same magnificent effect on you.

In these check-ins, ask yourself these questions:

- How do I feel right now?
- What do I need right now?
- What do I desire right now?
- How can I serve myself better?

Sometimes it's a sacred cup of tea, a meditation, a nap, or a good laugh that can make all the difference for you in how you feel in the small spa hotel called your new day.

So shift yourself to BE and live in your high-for-life frequency by checking in on yourself. Often.

That IS happiness!

Day 34

Mindfully present!

Being present means you are aware of - and focused on - your now. "I am here. Doing this. Right now!"

Being mindful means "I see, hear, taste, smell, think, and hear what is right now!"

Think about it... Right now I am here in my new morning. I am sitting in my living room hanging out with my cats. I am aware and present in this moment.

Versus... Right now, I am here in my new morning. I see my beautiful living room—it is a loving sight. I hear the vivid noises of nature. They are sounds of life. I smell fresh coffee. It is the smell of deliciousness. I taste this fresh coffee. It is a taste of magic. I scan my whole body, and feel every feeling there is for me—it feels peaceful. I consciously think thoughts of acceptance, respect, appreciation, gratitude, and love towards all that is for me, all that feels happy. This, right now, is a very sentient moment, in which I am mindful of everything.

Now combine *mindful* and *present* together, and you have magic on your hands!

Speaking of your hands, if you focus on your hands you are focusing on your now, because they are always doing whatever they are doing in the now. They pull you mindfully present into your now.

Make your new day a mindfully present one!

That IS happiness!

Day 35

Imagine a child looking up into the sky, saying "I believe...!"

There is so much magic, hope, love, and openness in this scene. Because the word "believe" and the action of believing in something carry the energy of hope, love, and magic to come. And a child carries the energy of pureness, newness, and magic. Feel this!

Now imagine you are that child, looking up into the sky, saying "I believe...!" Feel your immediate shift to BE and live in that same high-for-life frequency as that child.

In your new day, say or think "I believe...!" often:

- I believe that I am love and light.
- I believe that I am healthy and beautiful.
- I believe that I am deserving.
- I believe that I am giving my best, and that you are giving your best.
- I believe in magic and miracles.

Say it to others, "I believe in you!" This will shift you, and the person to whom you are saying it to, to BE and live in that frequency of goodness. And together as this believing team, you share this magic with everything and everyone around you.

Believing clears and cleans your energy, and it makes space for miracles and magic to happen.

That IS happiness!

Day 36

Are you chit-chatting all day long with what is in your awareness?

No?

You are missing out! Everything in your awareness has information to share with you, and is meant for you to engage with and learn from.

It is easy to do; simply speak out loud or think your *chitter-chatter*. You can ask whatever you like, and you can share whatever you want to share.

For example:

- Chit-chat with the water you are drinking about how to get in the flow, because water is really good at being in the flow.
- Talk with food to find which one is best for you.
- Converse with plants and nature about what you can learn from them.
- Talk with your house and see what it needs, or how you can serve it better.

Play with this and know that there are no limits.

Soon enough you find that everything wants to talk with you, and that you will never be lonely or bored again, because oh my, do these things love to chit-chat away.

That IS happiness!

Day 37

Imagine someone you love is asking you to do something for them. You get all excited and feel very special, important, trusted, and loved by their request. You go all out, and give your absolute best to do this for them with your purest love.

There is a lot of trust, appreciation, respect, gratefulness, happiness, and love created by them asking you!

Now imagine you asking your loved one to do something for you! Not so easy, is it? That is because you are programmed not to ask for help, but rather be strong and powerful and do it all yourself.

But think of all the high-for-life energies you are robbing yourself and your loved ones of, by not asking - or not letting them - help you.

So re-program yourself anew, and ask for help!

This can be as simple as asking a loved one to give you a massage, preparing you a bath, bring you tea, or reading a story to you. You can even ask them to do something that is their passion, like playing the piano for you.

Doing so will create a deep love and limitless good feelings... for you and your helper. And together, as this feel good team, you spread all that goodness to everything and everyone around you. Because everything is energy, connected, and shares their energy.

That IS happiness!

Day 38

Every rejection is a sign that the universe has your back.

Because if it is rejected, it is not the right happening, or the right time for you. It might also be that your mind wants it, but your heart says differently.

Of course, your first reaction can be anger, sadness, or hopelessness. Acknowledge those feelings, but refrain from diving into them too deeply. And certainly don't get hung up on the "why."

Rather acknowledge that the universe has your back!

If the reason for the rejection is not clear to you right now, it might be that you are not open to understand the "why" at this point. But know that soon enough you will be grateful, because there is something more fitting coming your way.

That keeps you resistance free towards what is happening for you right now. In that resistance free space, you can practice gratitude, which opens you up for what your heart really wants.

That IS happiness!

Day 39

Imagine sticking a spoon of honey into your mouth. Close your eyes and taste its sweetness. Feel this!

This imagination connects you to your own sweetness, because experiencing any sweetness means you shift to BE and live in your high-for-life sweet self.

So notice all sweetness in and around you:

- Sweetness in all smiles.
- Sweetness in flowers, smells, music, colors, and animals.
- Sweetness in desserts and drinks.
- Sweetness in everything and everyone making you think and feel "sweetness."

Use sweet words in all your conversations, and make sweet compliments to others. You shift them to BE and live in their frequency of sweetness too, which they will share with you, because you and them are connected.

In your new day, play around with sweetness and be creative in thinking, tasting, smelling, hearing, seeing, and feeling "sweetness" everywhere.

And for heaven's sake, go have that sweet treat you have always wanted!

That IS happiness!

Day 40

Feel pleasure!

Pleasure is like a very complex, potent, and delicious smoothie. Its ingredients are multiple good energies and feelings, like happiness, enjoyment, and positivity, all combined together in one word.

Everyone can feel pleasure, but it is very unique and different for everyone.

Waking up can be a pleasure. A yummy meal can be a pleasure. Laughter, enjoying a sunset, favorite book, or music can all be pleasure. Romance can be pleasure. There is so much to choose from.

So ask yourself what is *pleasure* for you? Then go all-out in your new day, and create your own unique world of pleasures.

Also, look around you: see, hear, taste, smell, think, and feel what pleasures are going on for others. Tune into them and enjoy their pleasures with them.

And finally, ask yourself what pleasures you can create for others that are in need of pleasure. Surprise them, and enjoy pleasure with them.

Last but not least, there is always the sky, and that is a pleasure to look at 24 hours a day!

That IS happiness!

Day 41

Imagine you are waking up to your new day! Your body, mind, soul, and consciousness are all fresh and clean.

Pause!

Right then and there you have a chance to set the desired tone for your new day with your first thought. So use this important moment to your advantage, and set your wanted flavor, because that clarity is a manifesting super-producer! It sets the stage for how you want it to be, and then shifts you to BE and live in that high-for-life frequency.

If you know your desired tone right away, set it, and get ready for your new day to be as you wish.

If not, ask yourself, "How do I want my new day to be?" Take the first words that come to your fresh mind, and set your intentions.

For example, if you set the tone that your new day already is - and will be - a light and happy day, notice how you give your whole being and your new day instructions: to be happy and light. Feel your immediate shift to BE and live in that light and happy frequency. This makes for a light and happy day.

Use the momentum of waking up (also after a nap!) to create your perfect day!

That IS happiness!

Day 42

"I wonder..."

What a bundle of magic these words are!

They initiate imagination, creativity, hope, change, adventure, possibilities, *open-ness*, compassion, and awareness. "I wonder..." also shifts you to BE and live in a frequency of awe. And being in awe opens you to receive magic, miracles, and wonders.

Below are some powerful examples:

- I wonder what my new day will bring? This creates openness and flexibility.
- I wonder what it would be like to fly? This creates imagination and creativity.
- I wonder what that person feels and needs? This creates compassion and kindness.
- I wonder what I should do today? This creates adventure, possibilities and activates all new.
- I wonder what I should create next? This creates change, newness and opportunities.
- I wonder what my heart would love to do? This brings you closer to your heart.

In your new day, go all-out and wonder ahead, and just keep wondering.

That IS happiness!

Day 43

Imagine yourself entering a small crystal and gem store.

The walls of the whole store are covered in a displays of sparkly healing stones. There is a swivel chair in the middle of that store space. You go and sit down in that chair. You take a spin so you can see all the gems and crystals, on all four walls. You are in awe of all the beauty that is there and available for you to see, think, hear, smell, taste, and feel.

You can choose to experience all beauty that is there and available for you in your life right now, in that same feeling of awe.

So have a seat in a swivel chair in the middle of where you are, and take a spin. If you don't have a swivel chair, stand and twirl yourself around. See all beauty and goodness that is there for you.

For example:

Look at all the people around you: kids, spouses, friends, and co-workers. See, hear, smell, taste, think, and feel their kindness, love, and fun attitudes.

Look at all nature around you... or if you are in a busy city, look at all the activity around you. See, hear, smell, taste, think, and feel all the beauty and joy there is for you.

No matter if you just imagine it, really spin on a swivel chair, or twirl while standing, practice this often in your new day. Because becoming aware of all beauty shifts you to BE and live in your high-for-life frequency.

That IS happiness!

Day 44

A joyful life is created by practicing to be amused by all. Because...

"There is nothing ever serious enough to be serious about, but there is always everything amusing enough to be amused by." This is a thoroughly tested quote by yours truly!

At one point of too much frustration I simply came to the conclusion that there has to be a better way to react. I decided to practice to be amused by what I am frustrated about.

So...

When my kids were little, every time they spilled something or made a big mess, I smiled and said "You just fed the fairies!" That made us all giggle, and we were amused by the spill. A truly high-for-life frequency to be in. It worked, and is still working today... when we feed the fairies.

It really all depends on how you want to feel, how you look at it, how you think about it, and how you react to everything and everyone.

In your new day, look for your amusement in everything and everyone, focus on it, and fill yourself to the brim with this fun energy. Laugh, smile and joke around all day long!

And then see what happens!

That IS happiness!

Day 45

What or which irritation-angel is in your face?

Every un-fitting person or happening (both are irritation-angels) gives you the possibility to think, see, hear, taste, smell, and feel what you are ready to experience. They gift you with the opportunity to clean out, heal, and let go of all that is no longer fitting. With that, renew yourself and get to know yourself better and better.

So don't be angry or resist your irritation-angels. Rather, welcome them and show gratitude towards them, because what you feel is yours to feel.

They are simply gifting you with their presence.

If the irritation-angel is a loved one, you can thank them even more, because with being in your face all the time, they are making sure you constantly feel their presence. That means you will never forget to embrace their energy and love, for the gifts they are, and keep co-creating beauty together.

In your new day, say "Thank you!" to all your irritation-angels that show up for you!

That IS happiness!

Day 46

Imagine a colorful, super-sized balloon that you get to fill with all your wishes, dreams, and desires!

Go all out and don't hold back… Think, say, feel, and visualize all you wish for. Wish for your personal desires and wish for other people's desires as well. Wish for earth's desperate desire for peace, hope, trust, kindness, love, healing, and happiness. Fill your super balloon to the brim!

Then with a smile, untie it and let it fly high up into the sky. Knowing with excitement that once it is at the perfect height, it will pop. Showering you and the whole world with your wishes, dreams and desires. Feel this!

Everyone has wishes, dreams and desires! Holding them hidden suppresses a huge part of you, which creates resistance. And that resistance will never go away, because in your heart you always know what your wish, dream or desire is.

If instead, you constantly focus on them and send them generously out into the universe, you shift to BE and live in a high-for-life frequency, because that is what your wishes, dreams, and desires are made of. Plus think about it: you are showering yourself and everything with all that goodness, shifting the whole world to BE and live in a magnificent frequency!

And imagine what would happen if everyone filled their balloons once a day, let them fly and, pop! The whole world, showered in magic!

So send them out in big heaps, and very often! And tell everyone to do the same.

That IS happiness!

Day 47

The good goose bumps!

You know the ones you get when you listen to a beautiful and moving song, or see a breathtaking scenery? Those are the "good goose bumps" that I am talking about.

These good goose bumps carry an energy of excitement, beauty, aliveness, and healing. They are like a powerful light beam of good feelings, going straight into your heart.

So make it a priority to create as many good goose bump moments as possible in your new day. Experience them consciously and really feel, see, hear, taste, smell, and think of all these good feelings filling your heart. Shifting you to BE and live in your high-for-life frequency.

Good goose bumps are an amazing experience, and so easy to spark.

Go for them!

That IS happiness!

Day 48

Imagine you are saying "NO" to something or someone that is not fitting or feeling good to you!

Are you really saying no to *it* or *them*? Or is what you are actually saying, a nice big "YES" to yourself?

I believe in the latter. And I want you to go out there in your new day and say lots of "Yeses" for yourself. The more you say "YES" to yourself, the cleaner and fitting your environment and time, your physical body, mind, soul, and consciousness become. And all that *clean-ness* shifts you to BE and live in your true high-for-life frequency of happiness and health... which you then can share with everyone and everything around you, spreading all that goodness wider and wider.

You make the world a better place by being true and saying "YES" to yourself!

That IS happiness!

Day 49

Do you ever feel you have to shift yourself into a certain way of being or behaving in order to do something?

For instance, you need to become still in order to meditate. You need absolute quiet to write or read something. Or you need a certain mindset to be able to do your work or talk to someone?

Do you also feel exhausted, stressed, or even nervous, because of this shift needing to take place? You might even ask yourself, "What if this shift is not happening, then what?"

Relax! The only shift you need, is your shift to be and live in your heart!

Because when you are in your heart, you're automatically aligned with who you really are. There, your connection to your teammates (your body, mind, soul, and consciousness) is strong and clear. Your wisdom can flow, and the support of the universe can reach you. You can simply be and do everything as your natural limitless you. No exhaustion, no stress, and no nervousness.

Plus! Don't forget you are never doing anything alone. Ever! You are always co-creating with your body, mind, soul, consciousness, and the universe. So, lean on them.

The easiest way to arrive in your heart is to focus on - and feel - your beautiful breathing. Once there, you will naturally be in the perfect energy and behavior you need to do anything.

Just think about it:

- You can meditate from your heart while walking without even needing to be still.
- You can write from your heart without even thinking.

- You can work from your heart without being exhausted and nervous.
- You can talk to others from your heart with staying true to yourself.

Be and live in your heart!

That IS happiness!

Day 50

Just as a simple and basic meal of eggs sunny-side-up and toast (or any other simple meal) can bring so much comfort and happiness, a simple and basic life attitude can bring you comfort, peace, love, light, and happiness too.

So be simple in your new day and practice any or all of the following:

- Slow down, be present, observe!
- Hear, see, taste, smell, think, and feel!
- Exercise and move your body!
- Eat clean food!
- Drink plenty of water!
- Meditate!
- Laugh and play!
- Be in awe!
- Sleep and rest!

Focus on all the good and see the gift in all. Practice appreciation and gratitude. Serve and help others. Love yourself and all.

Simplicity is comfort!

That IS happiness!

Day 51

Imagine that you have a "Magical Blessing Wand."

With that wand, you get to bless everything and everyone you encounter in your new day. Once touched by your blessings, miracles can happen.

Your outspoken well-wishes to yourself, something, or someone, are like that "Magical Blessing Wand." They touch hearts and make miracles possible. They shift you and others to BE and live in a high-for-life frequency and together, as this blessed team, you spread this goodness to everything and everyone around you; because everything is energy, connected, and shares its energy.

Be that powerful "Magical Blessing Wand" waver, and generously send your well-wishes out into the world.

That IS happiness!

Day 52

Have an intention-setting "chit-chat" with yourself when you wake up!

Ask yourself, "What and how do I want to feel today?" Keep it simple and trust the first word you hear.

Set your intention to feel accordingly. Think or say your intended feeling. Write it in a journal if you like, because when brought to life on paper, it intensifies your intention.

Next, close your eyes and visualize yourself feeling as you intend to. See, hear, smell, taste, think, and feel how happy you are to BE and live in this feeling. Stay here as long as you wish. This practice shifts you to BE and live in the high-for-life frequency of your intended feeling.

Now go live and experience your new play-day, all guided and supported by your intention. Once in a while, check in with yourself, and become mindful of how you are feeling. Is it still fitting with your set intention?

If so, then keep rocking your day, you are doing fabulously!

If not, shift back into your intended feeling, with traveling back in time to your morning "chit-chat" and visualization. Feel it and relive it fresh.

And there you have it, you arrived in your intended feeling again.

That IS happiness!

Day 53

Imagine you are watching a good drama movie.

You lose yourself in it, and feel the drama with every cell of your body, mind, soul, and consciousness. When the movie is done, you are a bit drained and exhausted. It takes you a while to regain balance and shift back to BE and live in your frequency of feeling really good. You are happy you watched it, but decide that a drama movie is not for every day.

Drama carries the energy of unbelievable, intense, extreme, severe, unreal, unhealthy, and un-happy.

Indulging in feeling, seeing, hearing, smelling, tasting, and thinking of any drama - be it yours or that of someone else - shifts you to BE and live in that dramatic frequency. A draining and exhausting place to be.

Versus...

Indulging in feeling, seeing, hearing, smelling, tasting, and thinking of any happiness (be it yours or that of someone else) shifts you to BE and live in a happy frequency. An energizing and nourishing place to be.

Drama is always present and available in every split second, but so is happiness. I urge you to enjoy all happiness and leave indulging in drama for a drama movie once in a while.

Make your new day a drama-free zone!

That IS happiness!

Day 54

What do you love right now?

Ask yourself this question first thing waking up, once every hour in your new day, and last thing before you fall asleep. Set a love-alarm to remind you!

When the alarm goes off, choose something or someone that you love right then and there. Say - or think - "I love...!" Feel, see, hear, taste, smell, and think of loving the chosen one or thing. Practicing this shifts you to BE and live in a high-for-life frequency of love, which you can nourish yourself with for the next hour.

When the alarm goes off again, choose something or someone different that you love right then and there. Say or think it, and feel it!

Your choice of what or whom you love can be for the sun, a coffee, or song. Your chair or your comfy pillow, a smile or a loved one. Whatever sparks your love at that moment is perfect.

Make this a routine, because it shifts you to BE and live in a frequency of love all day long.

That IS happiness!

Day 55

Imagine a beautiful and delicious apple!

That apple is an apple! It grows like an apple, looks and behaves like an apple, tastes like an apple, and it successfully enchants everyone as an apple. The apple is true to it being an apple, and that is why it successfully can shine bright and tasty, as an apple.

That is how nature works!

Think how this apple would fail its growth, looks, and taste, if it would pretend to be a lemon, or compare itself to a lemon. And let's not even start to discuss how disenchanting that apple - pretending to be a lemon - would be.

Well, you are nature too!

You might be an apple, or you might be something completely different. Either way, you can only shine your light bright and enchant the world if you are true to your unique "who" you are.

You are one of a kind! You are made up of your beautiful physical body, your smart and fun mind, and your glorious soul and consciousness. You come with happiness, love, peace, health, positivity, and joy, just as you come with anger, sadness, fear, jealousy, and negativity. All of it together is you; and it is all beautiful. Not to mention how boring it would be to miss any part of you.

So accept, respect, appreciate, thank, and love all of you, and be the apple or whatever else you are 100%.

That IS happiness!

57

Day 56

Sharing is caring!

Sharing is an act of the heart and it has the power to open, nourish, and heal hearts. When you share you shift yourself, who you share with, and what you share, to BE and live in the high-for-life frequency of the heart.

Sharing is also how our universe naturally works, just think of the fact that we are all energy, connected, and share our energies at all times. It never goes against the natural flow and has the added benefit of touching hearts.

So what could you share today?

A smile, a hug, a compliment, kindness, compassion, appreciation, gratitude, laughter and happiness, your time, thoughts or feelings, your heart and love, your listening ear or wise words, your lunch, a story, a joke, your success and knowledge, clothing, a blanket, your home, car, money, or help in other ways.

Be generous and make it a sharing, caring day!

That IS happiness!

Day 57

Imagine a loving parent!

They can be human or animal. Visualize how that parent serves their children and family with help, love, kindness, gifts, happiness, compliments, nice words, and care. Feel, see, hear, smell, taste, and think of all the goodness there is, in their serving.

Serving others carries a bundle of wonderful energy, and shifts you and the one you serve to BE and live in a high-for-life frequency. Add kind sayings like "I love serving you!" to your acts of service, and you double the effect of feeling good for you and the one you serve.

And together, as this good feeling team, you spread this powerful energy to everything and everyone. Because everything is energy, connected, and shares its energies.

Your service makes the world a better feeling place.

That IS happiness!

Day 58

Is there "a good use and need" for it?

As we all know - from lots of experience - there are many different kinds of feelings. There is love, anger, frustration, joy, sadness, jealousy, happiness, resentment, and peacefulness, to name a few.

They are all part of us, and it is important to acknowledge them and accept, respect, appreciate, thank, and love them. No exceptions!

But when we start feeling a lower vibration emotion, like anger, is there really "a good use and need" for us to fully and completely indulge in feeling it? Or would it be better to simply acknowledge, accept, respect, appreciate, thank, and love that feeling, without being eaten up by it?

We feel in the moment and lots of times when we look back, we find that there was not "a good use and need" for us to feel it wholly. The result being that it did not help us in our body, mind, soul, or consciousness. And, sometimes, the recovery time is huge.

So when you start feeling anger, pause, and ask yourself, "Is there a good use and need for me to really feel this? Or would it be better for me to simply acknowledge, accept, respect, appreciate, thank, love it for being a part of me, and move on with a happy dance?"

Depending on your response, either feel it to the extent that feels good for you (without hurting yourself or your surroundings), or move on to "a good use and magnificent need feeling" that serves your body, mind, soul, and consciousness better.

That IS happiness!

Day 59

Imagine that you cover all your floors with glitter! Now take a comfy chair, seat yourself in the middle of this glittery mess, and admire all the shimmer and shine. See, think, taste, smell, hear, and feel this brilliant energy filling every cell of your body, mind, soul, and consciousness.

Glitter carries the energy of magic, light, pretty, beautiful, *otherworldliness*, wonderfulness, and playfulness. When you notice it, it shifts you to BE and live in that high-for-life frequency.

There are millions of glitter moments to admire in your new day:

- In water drops, sunshine, and the sky.
- In stores and in your home.
- In smiling eyes.
- In makeup and clothes.

I promise you that with being enchanted by them, you will fill yourself a million times with that wonderful energy. And you will find that it actually is a pretty sparkly world out there.

So go on your glitter search mission, and become a *glitterologist*!

That IS happiness!

Day 60

Think of what a BFF does for you! A BFF makes your heart happy and nourished. They make you feel supported, loved and beautiful. They create a team with you, only want the best for you, and are always there for you.

Think what you do for a BFF. You are supportive and create a team together with them. You are loving, understanding, listening, attentive, and patient. You only want the best for your BFF and you are always there, no matter what.

Your food and you are meant to be BFFs! Food is meant to support you, nourish you, and to make you feel happy, loved, and beautiful. Food is meant to create a team with your physical body, only wanting the best for you, and to always be there for you. In turn, you are supposed to support your food and create a team together. Be loving, listening, understanding, attentive, and patient with it. Wanting only the best for it, and to always consciously be there with your food.

- Is this the exchange you create with what you eat?
- Is this how you feel about the food you are eating?
- Is the food you are eating bringing these BFF qualities into your body?

Thinking of and treating the food you indulge in as your BFF means you make eating a beautiful exchange, filled with gratitude, love, support, and nourishment. Which is only fitting, for such a sacred and healthy happening in your life.

That IS happiness!

Day 61

Imagine that you are in an elevator going up!

You are aware of the elevator climbing, higher and higher. You feel this uplifting feeling, and with that shift to BE and live in an uplifting frequency.

The word elevator carries the energy of uplifting, elevating, and ascending higher and higher. Now think of what an elevator does; it lifts you up to where you want to go. That action carries the energy of uplifting, higher, elevating, and ascending.

Riding an ascending elevator is 2 times the uplift, because of the word "elevator," and its act of elevating. And since everything is energy, connected, and shares its energies, that ascending elevator shares its uplifting energy with you. Given that you are aware, open, and receiving to this feeling.

In your new day, notice that every time you enter an ascending elevator, you are given an opportunity to shift to BE and live in that uplifted frequency.

I bet that you are excited to go *elevator-ing* today!

That IS happiness!

Day 62

Are you not sure anymore? If so, take a timeout!

Go inward—breathe and recharge. Remind yourself of the reasons you decided to do what you are doing, when your decision was all new and fresh. What were your thoughts and feelings back then?

If your original reasons still fit, close your eyes and re-feel the original thoughts and feelings you had at that time. Lose yourself in them! And on you go; doing what you are doing, re-charged and re-filled with all these high-for-life feelings of being sure.

If your original reasons do not fit anymore then ask, "Can I change these reasons to new and better fitting ones?" If the answer is "Yes," keep doing what you are doing... just adjust your reasons.

If you are still not sure, ask yourself "Is what I am doing still fitting for me?" If not, a shift to a new and better fitting "doing" is in order. Make a change!

And be assured...

It is a beautiful thing when you realize your reasons or what you are doing is not fitting anymore. Because it shows that you are growing and changing with the natural flow of your life.

BE and live, ever growing and ever changing!

That IS happiness!

Day 63

Imagine a beautiful wedding.

The bride and groom are on the dance floor, dancing. They are surrounded by all the guests, making this event their celebration. Nothing and no one are more important on this day than the couple. They are the center of their wedding and in the spotlight of their happiness gathering. What a sacred time!

Your new day is that happiness gathering for you, and you are the center of it.

So take that dance floor that is yours to take. Dance in the center of your new day. Enjoy being surrounded by all guests making it your celebration of your life. Feel, see, hear, taste, smell, and think of all *new-ness* that is ready for you to experience. What a sacred time!

And remember to return the favor with making this new day a sacred celebration for others too.

This is your day! BE and live it in a high-for-life frequency.

That IS happiness!

Day 64

"I am caressed!" Caressed comes with an energy of gentle, loving, sweet, taken care of, and touched.

Seeing, feeling, hearing, smelling, tasting, and thinking that you are caressed by everything in your new day, fills your tank of self-love, and shifts you to BE and live in a high-for-life frequency.

There are a million caressing opportunities for you:

- I am caressed by all the loving words in this book.
- I am caressed by the sun warming my face.
- I am caressed by the wind blowing around me.
- I am caressed by the rain getting me wet.
- My body is caressed by the water and food I ingest.
- My skin is caressed by the clothing I wear.
- I am caressed by my blankets while I sleep.
- My feet are caressed by the shoes I wear.
- My ears are caressed by the sounds of music.
- My nose is caressed by the scent of flowers.
- My eyes are caressed by all the beauty I see.
- My taste buds are caressed by all delicious tastes.
- My mind is caressed by all my happy thoughts.
- My whole being is caressed by all the high-for-life feelings I feel.

Shift to this wonderful frequency, with your focus on being caressed in your new day.

That IS happiness!

Day 65

Imagine your favorite car.

See it and feel how much you admire and love it. Think of all the different parts your favorite car is made of. Some are visible and make the amazing look of that car, while others are *not* visible and might not be that attractive to look at. But it takes every part to make this favorite car of yours, and you love them all.

Now think of yourself.

You are made up of all kinds of different parts, thoughts, and feelings. Some are visible and make your amazing looks, and some are *not* that visible and might not be what you want others to see. But it takes every part of you to make up your amazing being.

So acknowledge, accept, respect, appreciate, thank, and love all your parts by:

- Looking at yourself in the mirror and say to every part of you "I love you!"
- Acknowledging every thought you have, and say "I love you!"
- Feel every feeling freely, and say "I love you!"

Doing these will release any resistance you have towards any part of you, which makes space for you to love yourself as a whole.

That IS happiness!

Day 66

"Honor" is your magic for the day!

The word "honor" carries the energy of respect, celebration, being regal, and sacredness. Honoring yourself shifts you to BE and live in that high-for-life frequency. And when you say, "I honor you!" to others, you shift them to BE and live there too.

When you witness others being honorable they share their honorable energy with you, and when you notice the word honor in written form, you fill yourself with the goodness of honor.

In your new day, say or think:

- *I honor* my new day and my life.
- *I honor* myself and my body.
- *I honor* you and our friendship.
- *I honor* my work and chores.
- *I honor* everything and everyone.

Feel this! Be a being of honor!

That IS happiness!

Day 67

Imagine a gray and rainy day!

For some, that day feels like a very un-happy day and for others, that day is filled with happiness. Same day, same happenings, yet very different experiences.

However, both sides do have something in common; they are basing their happiness or un-happiness on something that is happening outside of them.

Not only is that not your pure happiness or un-happiness, but it is also exhausting and fairly impossible to stay or become happy that way. Because all it takes is for the rain to get stronger or stop, and your state of un-happiness or happiness changes. You have no say in it.

If you choose to be and live happy without needing a reason, not only does that mean you can always be happy, it also means you are in control of your happiness and un-happiness.

So shadow yourself in your new day, and become aware of what and whom you base your happiness or un-happiness on. Shift yourself to BE and live in your high-for-life frequency of being happy, simply because you are.

That IS happiness!

Day 68

Today is the day!

For me to go deep and BE what I truly am.

- Today is the day for me to BE my breath.
- Today is the day for me to BE in my flow.
- Today is the day for me to BE my peace.
- Today is the day for me to BE my love and light.
- Today is the day for me to BE my happiness.

Add to this list what fits for you. Rehearse and feel often in your new day.

Let any thoughts and feelings that are showing up for you while practicing your words come freely. Acknowledge them without judging. Accept, respect, appreciate, thank, and love them for the gift they are. Then let them go with ease and embrace the grounding that just took place.

Smile, breathe, and enjoy!

That IS happiness!

Day 69

Imagine this is what happens when you leave your house in your new day:

You walk to your car and spot a heart-shaped leaf. When you drive down the road, you see a heart-shaped sign in a window. When you go to lunch, you notice a heart-shaped chocolate. When you get back to work, you find a coworker with a heart on their shirt. When you leave work, you see a heart-shaped cloud in the sky. And when you get back home, your family gives you a card with a heart on it. Feel all these hearts!

Every heart carries the energy of love, gratitude, warmth, abundance, health, and happiness.

So every time you notice a heart, pause! Consciously acknowledge and feel that beautiful sign that is meant for you to experience! That shifts you to BE and live in your frequency of your heart, and it reminds you to be and stay in your heart.

Embrace every heart popping up for you!

That IS happiness!

Day 70

This is a love message from the universe:

Dear shining, powerful star, uniquely intelligent and magical being,

I want to tell you that you are a majestic, beautiful, powerful, kind, limitless, and rich being. That you are enough - lovable and perfect in every single way - as is.

- *I want you to look and focus on your grandness and amazing-ness.*
- *I want you to feel your majestic heart and live all the joy and bliss you create with it.*
- *I want you to understand that you are deserving, appreciated, and loved.*
- *I want you to indulge in your amazing journey with enjoying your sweetness inside of you.*
- *I want you to live and focus in your abundance.*
- *I want you to choose to shift yourself to BE and live in a high-for-life frequency of your truth.*

What is real is your love and light inside of you, and your happiness you create and manifest with that love and light. That is the only truth there is, and it is all yours to enjoy! Bathe in that love and light of yours, fill yourself with your happiness, and share it with everyone and everything around you. Enjoy your new day with smiles and giggles,

Your Universe!

That IS happiness!

Day 71

Imagine sitting on the deck of a cottage.

Suddenly, a fox runs by. He stops and stares at you. You both have a co-creating moment together. Then, he keeps on running through the land belonging to the cottage. Fox magic happened, just like that! You are in awe, and feel that this fox gifted you with a "Wow!" moment. What an experience!

Every split second of your life has "Wow!" moments like that in store for you.

A "WOW!" moment can be anything. From something huge, like giving birth, to something you do every day, like enjoying a delicious meal or receiving a compliment. It is very personal and different for everyone. But every "Wow" moment you think, see, hear, taste, smell, or feel has the same effect. It shifts you to BE and live in a high-for-life frequency.

So pay attention, and notice what gives you this "Wow!" feeling.

I guarantee you that there are millions of those "Wow!" moments happening for you in your new day, which means if you are conscious of them, you can fill yourself a million times with magic that is there for you.

That IS happiness!

Day 72

Every experience shapes you!

Constantly being shaped means you change, move forward, learn more about yourself, and become more and more your unique you. How cool is that?!

Invite and welcome all experiences (both, the ones you love and the ones you don't love) with openness and your best smile into your new day.

The experiences you love indulge in their delicious shaping of you. Feel your shift to BE and live in your high-for-life frequency of shaping up with happiness.

For the experiences you don't love: acknowledge, accept, respect, appreciate, thank, and love them for showing up for you. They are a gift to shape you closer to your truth.

And understand that you help shape everyone and everything around you as well. So be aware, and give your best to shape them well.

Enjoy shaping up!

That IS happiness!

Day 73

Today we build on yesterday, which was about shaping up...

Don't be sorry for anything or anyone!

Being sorry for someone who's experiencing something unpleasant or having a hard time, means you are sorry for them to receive the gift of shaping up, shifting closer to their truth, and moving forward in their journey.

Being sorry for them also means you create and fill yourself with sorry feelings, which are the opposite of high-for-life feelings. Filled up to the brim, you share your sorry feelings with the person you are sorry for, and spread it to everything and everyone around you. Which means you all shift far away from feeling good.

Instead, offer the uplifting support of your love, help, understanding, compassion, and kindness. Offer your belief and trust in them that they are capable of experiencing this shaping gift. Be a good listener without any judgements or attempts to fix it for them. And quietly - without voicing this to them - be excited for their opportunity to shape up and move forward in their journey. Lastly, visualize their powerful being with all their mightiness.

This will let them freely shape up with their experience, while being filled with your uplifting support. Shifting you and them to BE and live in a frequency of goodness, which you both will share with everything and everyone around you.

That IS happiness!

Day 74

Imagine you stand on the side of a busy road, and give every person that drives or walks by a flower and a smile.

Now imagine that the next day, you stand on the side of that same busy road and give every person a rotten tomato and a frown. Because that is all you have available to give and spread that day. Even though you know it is not as good as yesterday, you decide to give it anyways. At least you are giving something, today. Right?

Well, those will have two very different outcomes.

In one you spread positivity and happiness, and in the other you spread anything but positivity and happiness.

So be aware of your thoughts, feelings, words, and actions you have available to give and spread in your new day.

If you have positivity available, spread generously. That will create more, and it will come back to you like a boomerang.

If all you have is negativity, if you can, turn it into positivity before you give and share it with others. If you can't turn it into positivity, simply keep it for yourself without spreading and giving anything.

If someone spreads negativity, catch yourself before shifting towards their negativity. Either grow your positivity into an overflow, and share it with them to over-positive the situation, or remove yourself and your emotions without getting entangled with their negativity. In your thoughts send them love, and wait until the storm has passed.

That IS happiness!

Day 75

Pick an adjective that shifts you to BE and live in your high-for-life frequency!

Adjectives carry a certain energy, and using an adjective shifts you to BE and live in that certain frequency.

For example, take "sparkly!" Sparkly carries the energy of festive, light, joyous, happy, and magical. Every time you think, say, hear, see, smell, taste, or feel sparkly, you shift to BE and live in the frequency of sparkly.

Or think how different it is to hear, "Do you want dessert?" or "Do you want some of our deliciously decadent and specially homemade out-of-this-world dessert?" A huge difference, right?

In your new day, say or think your chosen adjective often and feel your shift to the wonderful frequency of that adjective. Say it to others and witness their shift to that frequency too. This goodness will be shared with everything and everyone, which makes your adjective spread wider and wider.

That IS happiness!

Day 76

Imagine you encounter a squirrel that is desperately trying to fly like a bird.

It keeps climbing up the tree and taking jump after jump, in the hopes that flapping its arms will make it fly. You realize that that squirrel clearly forgot who it really is and cannot succeed because of that. So you say to the squirrel, "Remember who you really are!" The squirrel looks at you, and suddenly realizes that because it forgot who it really is, life is hard.

The saying "Remember who you really are!" grounds you and shifts you back into your truth, to keep you honest to yourself. Especially if you encounter un-fitting happenings or people. Pause, then say or think, "Remember who I really am!" See hear, think, smell, taste, and feel your shift to BE and live in your truth. From that space you can react with what is true for you.

In your new day, say or think "Remember who I really am!" often, and bathe in your true light and love.

That IS happiness!

Day 77

Think of all the street and traffic signs!

They are always there and everywhere. They give clear directions on what to do and what not to do; where to go and where not to go, and they inform everyone how everything has to be, which creates great clarity.

Do you have your signs up?

Give clear signs to everything and everyone around you on how you want it to be and how you don't want it to be, on what you want and what you don't want. And give especially clear signs on what everyone can and cannot do.

You might even like to consider giving clear signs as to what happens when your traffic signs are disregarded.

With you having all your street and traffic signs up for everyone to see, clarity takes over and makes for a clear new day.

That IS happiness!

Day 78

Imagine a robot with no feelings.

It simply does what it needs to do, without feeling anything. It gets everything done in a very business-like way. A bit gray sounding, no?

Now imagine this robot can suddenly feel. So everything it does, is now accompanied by a feeling. Being just became very vivid and colorfully fun for that robot. It actually feels alive now.

I want you to practice being the robot with feelings!

- When you eat, feel how this food feels to you.
- When you put on clothing, feel how the clothing feels to you.
- When you put shoes on, feel how those shoes feel for you.
- When you walk down the street, feel how every step feels for you.

Also, ask yourself when you hug your family, how does it feel to you? Or when you enter your home, how does it feel to you? You might immediately say "it feels great", but that quickness is your mind and habit speaking. I want you to feel it!

Practicing "feeling" shifts you to BE and live in a vivid high-for-life frequency.

Your day becomes alive, and you get to know a lot about yourself while constantly asking yourself how things feel for you.

That IS happiness!

Day 79

Do you see fresh or rotten tomatoes? Because that determines your experience.

A few years back my family and I relocated to Italy. Our first short-term apartment was overlooking Europe's biggest open-air market located in a dangerous part of town, as we were told. Coming from New York City, that made us chuckle. As we arrived we watched the merchants having a great time yelling about their merchandise at this incredibly alive, busy, and gigantic market, right outside of our window. All we could see was the beauty of these many different fresh red tomatoes. We were in awe!

It felt amazing to wake up at 5 am with the noise of the market being prepared. And it was fascinating watching them clean up this big mess after the market closed, turning it into a huge open space where people parked their cars, walked, hung out and played soccer. Most important, we never encountered any danger and our wallets never got picked.

Then we had visitors, and even though they loved the experience of visiting Italy, all they could see was the trash, the mess, the noise, the chaos, and the danger. You can probably guess what happened to one of those wallets.

What was our bliss, was their non-bliss. Where we saw beautiful fresh red tomatoes, they saw rotten tomatoes. All in the same place and in the same time, with both fresh and rotten existing. Yet because our personal perceptions were dissimilar, the experience was completely different. Find, see, and focus on the fresh tomatoes in your life!

That IS happiness!

Day 80

Imagine a soft and gentle blanket.

Picture yourself touching it. Feel that softness and gentleness. Now roll yourself into that blanket of goodness. Are you purring yet?

You have that same softness and gentleness in your heart! Everyone does.

And you are that same softness and gentleness in your heart! Everyone is.

Feeling, seeing, hearing, tasting, smelling, and thinking of that softness and gentleness shifts you to BE and live in a frequency of your softness and gentleness. And since these energies are rooted in your heart, you shift to BE and live in your heart.

So focus on all that represents softness and gentleness for you:

- Put on soft clothes and soft shoes.
- Have a piece of soft fabric in your pockets to touch often.
- Pet a soft animal.
- Hug a loved one.
- Enjoy a soft and gentle foam bath.
- Enjoy soft and gentle foods and drinks.

In your new day, be soft and gentle to yourself and others. This makes for a cozy day!

That IS happiness!

Day 81

Gain clarity with a YES or NO day! That is a day where no "maybe," no "probably," no "perhaps," and certainly no "I don't know" phrases have any space to even exist.

Every choice, question, and decision you get to make in that day, choose to answer from deep within you with either a YES or NO. If you can't clearly say YES, it's naturally a NO. That cuts out a huge load of exhausting second-guessing, over-thinking, "what if" problem creating, and being stuck. Just imagine all the extra energy you will have available to be your crazy you! So ask yourself:

- Does this feel good for me, yes or no?
- Does this food energize me, yes or no?
- Do I want a piece of chocolate, yes or no?
- Am I happy, yes or no?

Take all that clarity you gain from your YES or NO day, and make the appropriate changes that are good for you.

Some happenings you can change right there on the spot. Some, you can initiate the change... knowing it is a process and it will take some time. And some, while you can't initiate a change right now, you can gain clarity that a future change is needed for your happiness. In the meantime, change how you perceive them, because that lets you say YES to them for now. And from there, you can focus your thoughts on how you want it to be, which naturally will strengthen the manifestation of change.

That IS happiness!

Day 82

Imagine eating a spoon full of ice cream!

But wait...

First look at that ice cream, and feel what it represents for you. What do you feel when you look at it?

Then smell the ice cream and feel what it represents for you. What does the smell make you feel?

Finally, feel what this ice cream represents for you when you indulge in it:

- What does the taste make you feel?
- What does the cold make you feel?
- What does the creaminess or iciness make you feel?
- What does eating this ice cream make you feel?

Enjoying your ice cream consciously turns this experience into a spa treatment for your feelings, because you get to feel, clean out, and create new feelings. Plus you also receive loads of information, knowledge, understanding, and wisdom about yourself.

Not to forget the great reminder in this—to melt into life and co-create with your life, just as this ice cream melted in your mouth and co-created this deliciousness with you.

Have your kids practice enjoying their treats consciously too. Not only will they think it is fun, they will also learn a lot about themselves and be more grounded because of it.

That IS happiness!

Day 83

Where does your power lay?

How many of the un-fitting happenings in your life are really your doing? And how many of them are someone else's doing with you simply caught in the middle of it?

Have a truthful look!

Without judging, but only gratitude, sort them into two imaginary beautiful gift boxes. Choose gift boxes because all un-fitting happenings (yours and not yours!) are gifts for you, to get closer to yourself. Label one "mine" and one "not mine".

If the unrest is truly yours then your power lays in changing and shifting back to BE and live in your high-for-life frequency. Acknowledge your unrest, accept, respect, appreciate, thank, and love it for the gift it is for you. Then shift back to your peace.

If the unrest is not yours, your power lays in staying in your peaceful frequency, without letting it shift you off your heart-path. You trust, believe, and know that the peace you are already in is right for you.

That IS happiness!

Day 84

Imagine you have pizza dough in your hands!

This dough is ready to be formed into a pizza shape. First you stretch it slowly in every direction. Then you stretch it more and more, farther and farther. Because you know that the more you stretch it, the smoother it gets, and the better the pizza dough will bake and taste.

That is the same for your physical body. The more stretched you are in your body, the smoother your experiences get, and the better your life will be, and feel for you.

A stretched physical body is also a healthy body, and a healthy body can create happy thoughts and feelings for you which shift you to BE and live in a high-for-life frequency. From there you can easily stretch yourself to leave your comfort zone of being to reach new ground.

Stretching carries the energy of movement, further ahead, new ways, and looser. When you stretch, you shift your whole being (body, mind, soul, and consciousness) to a stretched frequency. And that is a place of new possibilities.

So stretch often!

Plus! Notice all stretching around you, in people exercising, kids stretching while playing, a stretchy hair or rubber band, or a big smile stretching across a face. Feel, hear, smell, taste, think, and see those stretches. Doing so shifts you to BE and live in that amazing stretched frequency.

Make your new day a stretchy one!

That IS happiness!

Day 85

Clean out!

First, create a cleansing frequency by lighting a candle, preparing a delicious detoxing drink, putting on some cleansing sounds, and setting your intention consciously to a powerful cleansing time ahead. Feel this!

Then, *de-clutter* and clean-out your home. Go room by room through everything you have and lighten your home. Sort everything that you are parting with into two piles. One is give-away and one is recycling. Be generous with letting go. Feel this cleansing!

And while cleaning out your home, visualize cleaning out and *de-cluttering* your thoughts and feelings the same way. Sort them into two piles; a give-away pile, because they are not yours, and one to recycle—because they are not fitting you anymore. Feel the cleansing of your being with everything you let go of.

Once your big clean-out happens, consciously clean and let go of all that is not yours - or does not fit you anymore - right when it shows up for you, while hustling and bustling in your adventure of your new day.

This makes you feel clean at all times!

That IS happiness!

Day 86

Imagine yourself smiling while jumping on a trampoline.

Hear yourself laughing, feel how happy and silly you are, and think of how jumping energizes your body, mind, soul, and consciousness.

A trampoline carries an energy of playfulness, youth, joy, and fun. And jumping carries an energy of movement, being light, playful, youthful, and joyful. So naturally jumping or imagining yourself jumping on a trampoline shifts you to BE and live in a high-for-life frequency which you will spread to everything and everyone around you.

You can take this even further, and imagine that every new moment in your new day is a different trampoline that gets you jumping - from moment to moment, from experience to experience. With every jump you take, you fill yourself with high-for-life energy, giving you the superpower to make this the most playful, youthful, joyful, and fun day ever.

Jump! Go ahead, jump!

This IS happiness!

Day 87

Visualize your physical life as a garden that you get to design and seed as you like! Here is how it works:

- You have an unlimited amount and variety of seeds.
- You get to sow the seeds of your choice.
- You get to nurture those seeds as much as you like.
- You also get to weed all the plants you don't want in your personal garden.

It is your garden, your responsibility, and you decide the look, feel, smell, taste, and sound of it.

In this visualization, the seeds represent your thoughts, and the plants you weed out are your thoughts already manifested into happenings you don't want in your life. So, ask yourself:

- What thoughts am I choosing right now?
- What thoughts am I sowing right now?
- What thoughts did I already sow?
- What thoughts am I nurturing in my life?
- What happenings do I want to weed out?

Because it is your life, your responsibility, and you decide the look, feel, smell, taste, and sound of it.

Make sure your thought-seeds are of a healthy, happy, and abundant nature, because they make your life and create your future.

Thoughts are powerful seeds!

That IS happiness!

Day 88

Imagine a perfect resting place for you!

It can be a nice big bed, a quiet space in the woods, a sauna, or a boat on the ocean. Use the first picture that comes to your mind. Observe your resting place! Where is it? How does it look? What colors are there? Make it perfect for you, and get to really know it. Feel this!

Now visualize yourself entering your resting place through an entrance. Place yourself comfortably and close your eyes. Breathe and feel yourself relaxing and enjoying your peaceful rest.

In your new day, visualize and feel yourself going into your resting place often. A couple minutes here and there will do magic for you, because a rested body, mind, soul, and consciousness can shift to BE and live in a high-for-life frequency of happiness.

And create extra rest space in your new day with sleep, a tea break, a walk, a bath, yoga, sauna, or anything that means and is rest for you.

That IS happiness!

Day 89

Imagine that this is what happens when you walk up the stairs:

- With every step you take, you walk up and forward in what you want, and up and closer to yourself.
- With every stair you climb, you go higher and higher in your life. The higher you get, the happier you get.
- With every floor landing you reach, you get to leave something non-fitting behind. A happy good-bye indeed.

Not only do you shift to BE and live in your high-for-life frequency, but you also clean yourself and become lighter with this imagination.

Now imagine how much more potent this practice gets if you decide to really walk all the stairs in your new day while thinking and feeling yourself going higher and higher, and becoming lighter and lighter.

What are you waiting for?

Go climb these stairs of your life!

That IS happiness!

Day 90

Imagine that in your new day all you can see, hear, taste, smell, feel, and think is the word "calm."

"Calm" carries the energy of peaceful, quiet, balance, health, and the feeling that all is well. Saying, thinking, focusing on, and noticing all "calm" in and around you shifts you to BE and live in a frequency of calmness.

Breathe and feel these words:

- I am calm.
- Everything is calm.
- Everyone is calm.
- All is calm.

And...

- Feel your deep calmness in every breath you take.
- Feel your calmness in your body; organs, cells, your water and your blood.
- Feel all calmness in your food, tea, clothes, house, work, pets, in other people, and the sky.

Be your calmness in your new day!

That IS happiness!

Day 91

Think of the monkey bars at a playground!

You swing forward from bar to bar, hanging on tight with at least one hand until you have a firm grip on the following bar, then you let go and swing forward to the next. And so on.

Do the same with your happiness!

Be a happy monkey on a monkey bar. Swing forward, from happiness to happiness, keeping a tight grip on feeling one until you have a firm grip on feeling the next happiness. And so on.

In your new day practice one happiness swing at a time, and have a blast while you are at it!

That IS happiness!

Day 92

Imagine that you are at a play.

You are seated and very excited. The play starts and the whole crowd is immediately captured by all the happenings on stage. It is a true masterpiece! You and the crowd enjoy it immensely, and at the end there is endless clapping and even a standing ovation.

After the play everyone gets the chance to meet the actors, and everyone that was involved in making this play possible. You congratulate them, tell them how much you enjoyed it and thank them for creating this theater experience for you.

They all smile with happiness, and with laughter they tell you about some funny mishaps that happened during the play. You look at them in surprise and say, "I did not even notice. All I saw and focused on was the amazing story and play you super stars put on."

Pretend your new day is a play, and that you are the spectator of that play.

If all you see and focus on are the great happenings, amazing story, and play - that is there for you in your new day - and you don't even notice the mishaps, you will be captured by your new day. You will find that it is your masterpiece, and you will enjoy it immensely.

Focus on what is going right for you!

That IS happiness!

Day 93

Washing the dishes by hand, cleaning the toilet, or getting ready for a gala are all the same!

These are all experiences that are part of your physical life, and no experience has more value than the other. The value is only created by how you are doing something, by the state you are in, by how you think and feel about what you are doing, by how you perceive it, and if you are consciously present in what you are doing.

Since you have full power to change the state you are in, and to change your thoughts, feelings and perceptions, you are also in charge of the value of every experience. Here is a recipe for peak high-for-life experience value:

- Become present in your NOW!
- Acknowledge everything as is!
- Accept everything as is!
- Respect everything as is!
- Appreciate everything as is!
- Thank anything and everything for the gift that it is!
- Love everything as is!

Add a sprinkle of happiness, a squeeze of joy, a spoon of laughter, a pinch of playfulness, cups and cups of trust, and all your personal favorite flavors of life to this mix. Mix it all together and believe! Then go experience your new day while being in that high-for-life frequency. I promise you that every experience will be a high value one.

That IS happiness!

Day 94

Imagine two different people walking down the street on different sides.

One is simply just walking down the street. The other has a spring in their step.

You watch them both and feel their energy.

- Who has more fun?
- Who is happier?
- Who is more confident?
- Who is being and living as if everything is magical?

Having a spring in your step means you are walking with energy, happiness, and confidence which shifts you to BE and live your new day in a fun frequency.

So be aware of how you walk!

Walk with a spring, maybe even get yourself skipping down the street. Take it even further, and imagine everything and everyone around you with a spring in their step or skipping. Keep going, and visualize the whole world starting to walk with a spring in their step or skipping down the street.

Feel how this imagination and movement shifts you, everything and everyone, to BE and live in a high-for-life frequency, changing the energy of the whole world to happiness.

Be the start of this shift and share it with your kids, family, and friends.

That IS happiness!

Day 95

Shoes!

Besides shoes helping you walk and going to places, they are also very cool happiness helpers for you. Because every shoe carries a specific energy, and with wearing them consciously, you shift to BE and live in their frequency. For example:

- Running shoes carry the energy of being sporty, fast, light, and flexible. Wearing them shifts you to BE and live in that high-for-life frequency.
- Rain boots carry the energy of being dry, safe, and protected. Wearing them shifts you to BE and live in that frequency.
- High heels carry the energy of being elegant, tall, and confident. Wearing them shifts you to BE and live their frequency.
- Slippers carry the energy of being comfy, snuggly, and warm. Wearing them shifts you to BE and live in a homey frequency.

So depending on how you want to feel, ask what shoes would give you the feeling you desire.

If you are still home, consciously put them on for your new day. If you are already out and about, imagine the chosen shoes, feel them, and visualize putting them on.

There you have it, your wanted shift took place! Enjoy!

That IS happiness!

Day 96

Imagine someone spills a drink!

Usually they are in distress about this happening. Now imagine that you say to them "It is OK, it is all OK. Are you OK?" Hearing these words lets them relax, maybe even gets them to smile or laugh about their mishap.

The word "OK" carries an energy of resistance-free, peaceful, acceptance, respect for what is, and "I am fine, you are fine, that is fine, and all is fine!"

Saying or thinking the word OK shifts you to BE and live in that frequency. Saying it to others shifts them to be and live in that powerful feel-good frequency too. And together as this "OK" spreading team, you share this goodness with everything and everyone around you.

Use the following words often in your new day:

- I am OK!
- You are OK!
- That is OK!
- All is OK!

And lets be honest, who would not want to be the messenger of such great news that all is "OK!"

That IS happiness!

Day 97

Lose yourself!

At least every now and then, just for a bit. Because that opens up all "new and exciting" for you. And it keeps you flexible, spontaneous, and in a receiving state.

Here is my little story...

Once upon a time I came up with this great plan for my new day. It made sure I got everything done on time, without hurrying like crazy. All was great! Until my new day took my plan, crushed it, and recycled it into an even greater plan. That is when it all changed from great to magnificent!

Instead of my plan, I got to watch a *Quidditch* game, live, with real *muggles*. Promise, I am not making this up. Spontaneous fun was created!

And instead of my plan, I got to sit in a new beautiful cafe, by a window with a magnificent tree smiling at me, like it knew I was coming. Spontaneous inspiration was created!

Those are just two of the plan-changing fantastic experiences I was given during that whirlwind day. And the best was, I still got everything done, not on my terms, but with the universal flow that was best for me. Spontaneous excitement was also created!

You might not be able to be that flexible every day, I am not either. But on the days where you can, even only part-time, take the universe's offers and love for you and lose yourself in whatever it has in store for you.

Expect magic to happen when you say "YES" to getting lost!

That IS happiness!

Day 98

Imagine that you and your physical body are hanging out for a chat with a cup of tea. You talk about how things are going, what changes you are ready to make moving forward, what expectations there are, what works, and what doesn't.

Next imagine that you are hanging out with your mind for a chat with a cup of tea. You talk about how things are going, what changes you are ready to make moving forward, what expectations there are, and what works, and what doesn't.

Then imagine that you and your soul are hanging out for a chat and a cup of tea. You talk about how things are going, what changes you are ready to make moving forward, what expectations there are, what works, and what doesn't.

And lastly, imagine that you are hanging out with your consciousness for a chat with a cup of tea. You talk about how things are going, what changes you are ready to make moving forward, what expectations there are, and what works and doesn't.

Think of the deep connections you create, all the amazing information and clarity you receive, and all new and exciting planning that will be created in those chats. And envision all the goodness being shaped, when you act on all that new knowledge, understanding, and wisdom about yourself.

You will never need other opinions or solutions about how to live your life, if you get going with your chit-chats.

That IS happiness!

Day 99

Be a rebel! Actively do the opposite of what is, which you don't like as it is. The best news for you is that you already know how to do that, because you rebel like that multiple times every day. For example:

- When thirsty you drink water to be the opposite, which is not thirsty.
- When sweaty you take a shower to be the opposite, which is not sweaty.
- When hungry you eat food to be the opposite, which is not hungry.
- When tired you take a nap to be the opposite, which is not tired.

See, you are already a trained rebel! Use this rebel training to your advantage. Instead of staying in a not-feel-good energy, shift to BE and live in your high-for-life frequency with doing the opposite of what is, that you don't like as it is.

- If un-happy practice something that makes you happy.
- If sad think of something that makes you smile.
- If you are bored create something fun.
- If you are angry watch a peace documentary.
- If you are frustrated help and serve others.

Practice your *rebel-ness* in your new day often!

That IS happiness!

Day 100

Imagine that you are skydiving!

You jump out of that airplane and trust the parachute completely to open up for a safe landing. You trust the company which tested the parachute that they did a thorough job testing it. You trust the skydiving company that they keep their gear in safe shape, and if you jump with an instructor, you trust that he knows what he is doing to give you a safe experience.

Without all that trust you would not go skydiving, but *with* all that trust you have a fantastic experience.

Trust is a very powerful and potent frequency. When you trust in everything that is happening for you, distrust and fear have no space to exist, which means you will go for your desires and live vividly and fully. Practicing trust and saying or thinking "I trust...!" shifts you to BE and live in that high-for-life frequency. Here are some great examples:

- I trust that I am supposed to be where I am.
- I trust that I am in charge to change anything.
- I trust that everything is a gift and opportunity.
- I trust that I am capable.
- I trust in my happiness, my light, and my love.
- I trust in life!

And don't forget to notice all trust that is in everything and everyone around you, in others, and in nature. That shifts you to BE and live in that goodness too.

That IS happiness!

Day 101

Light a candle!

Right after waking up to your new day, when you are still fresh and clean with your thoughts and energy... go light a candle.

Light it consciously, in a ceremonial way that fits for you. Look at its light and feel it! Breathe, and fold your hands in front of your heart.

Now say your personal mantra for your new day. Speak freely from your heart. There are no limits, and it can be different every day. Simply keep it positive and make it feel good for you.

The following mantra is meant as an inspiration:

Hello my body, mind, soul, consciousness, and universe. Thank you for this new day—I am excited for it. I am well and happy. I love myself. I shine my light fully, and will make this the most beautiful day ever. I will do good for myself and all others. Thank you for all that already is and all that will be. I love my new day. And so be it!

Then get busy in your new magnificent play-day. Smile!

Lighting a candle is a very sacred and beneficial act. Together with your mantra, it sets the tone for your whole being as well as your new day. And that will support you in and out.

That IS happiness!

Day 102

Imagine your own happiness garden!

- What does it look and feel like?
- What people, animals, and situations fit in your happiness garden?
- How do you feel when you stand in the middle of your happiness garden?

These thoughts shift you to BE and live in your high-for-life frequency of your happiness garden. And you receive great clarity on how you want it all to be for you.

Plus, standing in the middle of your happiness garden grounds you in your happiness, which means you take every step, think every thought, say every word, and act towards everything and everyone from the middle of your own happiness garden.

What a wonderful way to experience everything and everyone!

And just like any garden: to keep it clean, weed it! Throw out the non-fitting and keep bringing in the new that fits and makes you feel happy right then and there.

Shift yourself into your happy garden with imagining this often.

That IS happiness!

Day 103

Being generous is a world changer!

The word "generosity" and the act of being generous carry the energies of giving, abundance, sharing, kindness, love, and compassion.

Being generous shifts you, the person you are generous to, and what you are generous with, to BE and live in a high-for-life frequency. You co-create goodness together, with the fantastic side effect of spreading it to everything and everyone around you, and wider and wider it spreads.

Generosity can be practiced in many ways, shapes and sizes...

With your smiles, laughs, hugs, and compliments, your kindness, happiness, assistance, making way for others, and sharing and giving all that you can.

Be especially generous with sharing your love and light, it creates abundant happiness for you and others.

That IS happiness!

Day 104

Imagine you have two ponds.

One is full of water lilies, while the other has only a few. Your friendly neighbor asks if you could share some with them, for their pond. You say yes. Which pond will you take them from? The one that is full of lilies, so it won't matter if you take some out? Or the pond with only a few, which would make it look empty?

In this imagination, the pond is you, and the water lilies represents the amount of energy you have.

If you share and give your energy to help others, while being the pond with not much energy, you will be empty after you give.

But if you share and give while being the pond full or energy, you can easily give and give, and still be full, energized and healthy after giving.

To grow more water lilies and nourish them to stay, practice absolute self-care, self-acknowledgment, self-acceptance, self-respect, self-appreciation, self-gratitude, and self-love. Grow them and let your pond over-flow, and from that overflow you can share and give to help others easily.

Take care of yourself and your energy first, and don't forget to admire your pond!

That IS happiness!

Day 105

Tune-in to your magic channel!

I love to pull into the slow lane on a multiple lane highway. Why? Well the good news is, it is not out of fear or lack of driving talent. I simply love to slow down to the tempo that feels good for me, which is in the speed limit range, but slower than most other hurried cars. Now don't get me wrong, I have somewhere to be too, but funny enough I always get to my destination in time, even though I slow down.

But there is more that I love about it...

Driving represents life to me. In both, driving and life, you have a starting point and a destination. And in the middle you have this amazing journey, packed with adventures, feelings, people, animals, nature, and all you choose it to be. With slowing down, I tune-in to my magic channel, where I get to see and experience it ALL!

In your new day, slow down! Detach from everyone's hurrying and let it all pass beside you. And then tune-in to your magic channel, where you get to experience all that is there for you, right now and right here!

That IS happiness!

Imagine letting your little sibling have the last cookie in the jar, even though you want it.

You smile and indulge in the happiness your sibling is expressing with getting that last cookie. This shifts you to BE and live in a high-for-life frequency, because it is a magnanimous act!

The word magnanimous means "great soul." It carries the energy of big-hearted, noble, and generous.

To be magnanimous towards yourself means you shift to BE and live in a frequency of big-hearted, noble, generous, and forgiving towards yourself. Treating others in a magnanimous way shifts you and others to BE and live there too. Which spreads this goodness to everything and everyone around you, because everything is energy, connected, and shares their energy.

In your new day, make it important to focus on all *magnanimousness* in and around you, and feel your shift to BE and live in your noble heart.

That IS happiness!

Day 107

Take every moment you can to look up into the sky!

Every time, look as though you are seeing it for the first time ever. Because you are!

The sky is an ever-changing scenery: what you are looking at right now, you see it for the first time. And with every new view, there is a new experience for you to receive, a new energy for you to shift to, a new perspective to gain, and a new feeling for you to feel.

Every time you look up, ask yourself "How do I feel looking at this sky?" Don't think hard and take the first feeling that comes up for you. Feel it freely and fully! Accept, respect, appreciate, thank, and love your feeling.

This re-awakens feelings in you, and in feeling them, you will either clean them out in a healing way, or you re-fill yourself with high-for-life energy. Either way, it is yours to experience.

Move through your new day and look at the sky as much as you can, so you can feel as much as possible.

That IS happiness!

Day 108

Imagine a flower in the wind!

This flower is open to all the different shifts the wind is giving it. It moves a little to the right, a little to the left, a little backward, a little forward. All with the wind! And even though, there is a lot of shifting, the flower does not break. It seems that the flower has enough trust in itself to be flexible and strong enough, to bend and spring back.

Pretend you are that flower! And the wind represents all that is happening for you.

Shift with your happenings, a little to the left, a little to the right, a little forward, and even a little backward. Just like that flower! And know that you can trust yourself to be flexible and strong enough to bend and spring back without breaking.

Welcome all happenings in your life, because they are here to shift and point you in the direction you need to be in.

Sometimes that new direction is what you expect, which makes it feel good because it is in your comfort zone. And sometimes the shift isn't what you had planned, which makes it not always feel good right off the bat. But, as soon as you bend with the shift, it gets the chance to change into something that does feel good for you.

That IS happiness!

Day 109

BE gigantically open!

Think about the Bowhead whale and his "biggest mouth in the world." He opens it fully and completely, to fill it to the brim with water that has all sorts of things in it. He then skims through that water as it flows through his gigantic mouth, looking and tasting for his nourishment: the plankton. Yum! And on he goes, again and again, opening his "biggest mouth in the world" wide and huge, to catch the most of what he likes.

Just like that ocean water with all sorts of things in it, life has all sorts of experiences in it too. Some are nourishing you towards your happiness, and some are not.

And just like that whale, in order to catch as much of what you like, you have to be gigantically open to receive, and then skim through all of what life offers you. Feast on all that you love and the rest, let it wash through and out of you, without even trying to digest it.

On you go, opening gigantically again and again, to catch and skim for the nourishment that shifts you to BE and live in your high-for-life frequency of happiness.

That IS happiness!

Day 110

Imagine you are walking on a path along the side of a beautiful and adventurous river. Suddenly there is a luxurious boat filled with energies of love, beauty, abundance, positivity, happiness, and health pulling right up next to you.

The boat is inviting you to jump on and take over the steering as the captain. It tells you that this is your luxurious, high-for-life energy boat, and as long as you are on it, you will BE and live in that great frequency. You can stay as long as you want and get off whenever you wish. All up to you, you are in charge and in control!

In this imagination, the river represents your beautiful and adventurous life. The path represents your comfort zone. And the luxurious boat represents a way you could float through your life.

Now what? You can either walk on the path along the side of your beautiful and adventurous life, experiencing everything through your comfort zone. Or you can hop on this luxury boat and float right down the middle of it, which is not your comfort zone, and it might get a bit wild, unknown, and foreign.

- Would you even have to think about it?
- Will you jump on, or not?
- And if yes, will you commit to make it a priority to absolutely never leave that high-for-life frequency way of living again?

Go take that jump!

That IS happiness!

Day 111

You are a shiner!

Shiners are people that shine their light bright no matter what is happening for them! I can spot them easily, because they are always striving to be and live as a happier being. They always share their bright light with everyone and everything around them. They light up the world!

You are officially a shiner! I know, because you are reading this book. You light up the world! Your light deserves the best care to stay shining, happy, and healthy. Here is how:

- Acknowledge, accept, respect, appreciate, thank, and love all that is there for you.
- Focus on your blessings.
- Meditate, and move your physical body.
- Eat clean food and drink plenty of water.
- Smile and laugh often.
- Surround yourself with people that light up the world, and shine together.
- Play with children. They are pure shiners.
- Be with animals and nature. They shine brightly. Just think of a firefly.

Light candles and be with their light. Notice all *shiny-ness* around you. This shifts you to BE and live in the frequency of your light. Be a determined shiner of your unique bright light! Why?

Because that is your natural state.

That IS happiness!

Day 112

Imagine an ever-moving squirrel!

Moving to the left and to the right, moving up and down, forward and backward. Moving fast and slow, and once in a while, dangling from a tree. Squirrels move all the time, and have so much fun!

Be like that squirrel and move all the time too, because life is an ever moving experience, and if you keep moving you move together with life in its natural flow.

- So, move your body and create flexibility.
- Move your mind to new thoughts and gain *openminded-ness*.
- Move your expectations and attract new opportunities.
- Move your eyes and gain a different view.
- Move your lips and say wonderful words.
- Move your routine and shake things up.
- Move to new territory and leave your comfort zone.
- Move your furniture around and create a new energetic vibe in your home.
- And, be aware of all movement in and around you.

That shifts you to BE and live in a frequency of movement, which is where all the fun is.

That IS happiness!

Day 113

Kindness changes everything!

One kindness towards yourself shifts you to BE and live in your high-for-life frequency.

- One kind thought towards yourself will change how you think.
- One kind smile towards yourself will change your energy.
- One kind word towards yourself will change your heart.
- One kind feeling towards yourself will change how you feel.
- One kind service towards yourself will change your day.

Kindness towards anything or anyone shifts whomever and whatever you treat with kindness, to BE and live in a kind frequency which will be shared and spread further and further.

Base your new day on kindness and ask yourself often, "What kindness can I create?"

And watch yourself and the world change!

That IS happiness!

Day 114

Imagine that you get to pick a super-power!

What will it be? A super-power to make others and yourself laugh or feel amazing? A super-power to serve others? To cook delicious food? Or the super-power of being and spreading happiness?

Time to pick and plan!

How will you use it for you? How can you serve others with it? How can it make your life, other's lives, and the world better?

Now go into your new day, knowing that you have your super-power available to super power yourself, everyone, and everything around you.

And just as an idea...

If your super-power involves a costume, feel free to visualize yourself all dressed up. Only you will know about the what and the why that has you giggling all day.

That IS happiness!

In any great working community, if one component is in an uneasy state, the other components who are feeling great take over, help out, and balance everything. That makes the community healthy and thriving.

You are a community of different components; connected and working together. You are your physical body, mind, soul, and consciousness. If one of your components is in an uneasy state, your other well components will happily help. If two are in an uneasy state, you still have two other well components. There is always help available!

If you have an uneasy component, acknowledge it without judgment. Accept, respect, appreciate, thank, and love it. Then move to acknowledge the others that are in a well state. Feel them, focus on and live in them, until your uneasy component is well again. That will balance your great community of "YOU."

For example:

If your physical body is in an uneasy state then feel, focus and live in your mind, soul, and consciousness. Take a physical break and rest! Think good feeling thoughts, feel your happy soul, and be present in your consciousness.

If your mind is in an uneasy state then feel, focus and live in your physical body, soul, and consciousness. Take a mind break while being still with your thoughts! Do sports and movement, feel your happy soul, and be present in your consciousness.

If your soul is in an uneasy state then feel, focus and live in your physical body, mind, and consciousness. Take a soul break, with being still in your heart! Do sports and movement, think good feeling thoughts, and be present in your consciousness.

If your consciousness is in an uneasy state then feel, focus and live in your physical body, mind, and soul. Take a consciousness break, with pausing in your now. Do sports and movement, think good feeling thoughts, and feel your happy soul.

Give all components of your great community the chance to help and thrive, because that creates a balanced and happy existence.

That IS happiness!

Day 116

Imagine someone standing at a street corner saying "Thank you!" to everyone and everything passing by. Feel the wonderful energy that is created with this happening.

The words "Thank you," carry the energy of gratitude, love, and appreciation. They are deep healing words, capable of healing hearts and relationships within seconds.

Saying or thinking "Thank You!" shifts you and the person you are thanking to BE and live in a high-for-life frequency. Together, as this good-feeling team, you share it with everyone and everything around you. Because everything is energy, connected, and shares its energies.

Notice "Thank You" where it's written, pause and feel these healing words. Focus on each and every "Thank you" said, given, and acted on by people around you. That shifts you to BE and live in that amazing frequency.

That IS happiness!

Day 117

Just as a house gets dusty and dirty and is in need of cleaning, your energy becomes impure and needs cleaning too.

Clean energy is thriving, happy, inspired, light, and energized. Just think how amazing a clean house feels, or how refreshed you feel after a shower. Wonderful!

Impure energy is heavy, un-happy, numb, tired, exhausted, and drained. It feels like a dirty house.

In your new day, clean your energy often with practicing:

- Conscious breathing
- Gratitude and appreciation
- Smiles, laughter, and playfulness
- Meditation, exercise, or sauna
- Detoxing foods and drinks
- Sleep and rest
- Time in nature
- Healing sounds

And just to keep things real, a good cry always cleans your energy.

Happy cleaning!

That IS happiness!

Day 118

Imagine a falcon!

Even though it is presented with opportunities to hunt and eat in every split second of its life, the falcon will not take every single one. Because hunting like a crazy bird would be exhausting, and it would be too much food. It only hunts when he is ready, hungry, or simply can't resist because it feels right and good.

You too are presented with many opportunities for all kinds of new experiences in every split second of your life. Taking every one of them would be exhausting and too much. Not to mention dangerous!

So how do you choose which ones to go for?

Follow your heart! Choose the experiences that feel right and good for you, when you are ready, hungry, or simply can't resist. These are the ones that will shift you to BE and live in your high-for-life frequency.

Let all others go by like passing cars on the freeway, without getting involved.

That IS happiness!

Day 119

"I say YES!"

Feel, hear, taste, smell, see, and think how saying these words shift you to be open and receiving.

Take it even further and say:

- I say yes to living my life!
- I say yes to my happiness!
- I say yes to being healthy!
- I say yes to love!
- I say yes to success and abundance!
- I say yes to inspirations!
- I say yes to___! Fill in the blanks.

The word "YES" carries the energy of willingness, commitment, openness, positivity, hope, excitement, and receiving. Saying, thinking, and feeling "YES" shifts you automatically to BE and live in that receiving frequency.

"YES" also removes any resistance or blockages you have towards what you say yes to. It lets go of fear, distrust, and disbelief, which opens you up wide to all that is there for you.

Saying "YES" means magic can exist and arrive for you!

That IS happiness!

Day 120

Imagine that you are looking at a field of lush green grass. All you can see, hear, smell, taste, think, and feel is that color green. Breathe deep and feel this!

Green carries the wonderful energies of balance, peace and harmony, growth and renewal. Consciously imagining, thinking, and seeing green shifts you to BE and live in the high-for-life frequency of green. Which creates equilibrium between your mind and heart, because it balances your emotions.

So go on a green search! Once you spot some, pause, look, and feel its energy.

All that is left for you to do is to enjoy your shift to BE and live in peace and harmony, because you just gave your physical body, mind, soul, and consciousness a color wellness session.

"Green-out" often in your new day!

That IS happiness!

Day 121

What can you fall in love with today?

- Your magnificent You?
- A beautiful flower?
- A gorgeous tree?
- The ever-so-powerful sky?
- A delicious tea?
- A mesmerizing scent?
- A happy smile?
- A vibrant song?

Consciously notice all new that is happening for you in your new day and ask, "What can I fall in love with?" Then think of all existing things that you already love. Ask, "Which one can I fall in love with all over again?"

Once you chose the who or the what, focus on feeling, thinking, hearing, tasting, smelling, and seeing your newly found or re-found love. That will shift you to BE and live in the frequency of falling in love over and over.

What a day full of love!

That IS happiness!

Day 122

Imagine you inherit a pair of pants from a loved one.

They fit size-wise, but *oh goodness*, the color and pattern is totally not you. However, you know that with inheriting and wearing them, you honor your loved one. So you decide you will wear them one day a week—can't be such a big deal. But it turns out that it is a big deal!

Because when you wear them, you don't feel good, right, or like yourself. And many happenings don't go right for you on those days. Whereas on the days when you don't wear them, you feel amazing and the same things go right.

Those pants represent anything in your life you do for others, but is not true for YOU.

So one day you say, "No more! I am going to do what is right and fitting for me! And I will find better ways to serve and honor others."

Those are very powerful words that carry the energy of "stop" and "enough," which makes them a turning point to betterment. Using them shifts you to BE and live in a powerful frequency - where you can create fitting changes for you - and that is the moment when you commit; to honoring yourself, to making it right for you, and to feeling good while being true to yourself.

Congratulations, you have arrived in your heart!

In your new day be aware of how you feel about what you do.

Is it right for you, or not?

That IS happiness!

Day 123

Celebrate a clarity-creating relationship with your opinions!

Opinions are a great clarity-creating tool. They help you get to know yourself better, and to see clearly where a change is in order.

So ask yourself often, "What is my opinion on this?" and form your fitting opinion. Take this clarity to heart and make fitting changes for yourself.

But be aware, it's of utmost importance to refrain from "negativing" with your opinions. For example:

Saying "I don't like this music, it's just not for me." is a great clarity-creating opinion. But, "UGH. I hate this band. The singer looks like he smells like feet. Why do you even like this? It's not even real music." shifts your opinion into a negativity-spreading judgment. And that is the complete opposite of a healthy opinion.

This is also a great practice for kids. Ask them about their opinions, so they can form their own fitting opinions early on, and find clarity for themselves.

Play around with this and enjoy *opinionate-ing* for yourself.

That IS happiness!

Day 124

Imagine you get to hug an animal that you have always wanted to hug, but normally could not.

Pick one that makes your day the most spectacular ever!

Now imagine your animal in its full glorious beauty right in front of you. Wow!

Consciously see, hear, taste, smell, think, and feel its energy. For example, if it's a lion feel the majestic power, or if it's a baby kitten feel the gentleness and softness. Breathe and feel this!

Now slowly move closer and hug your animal. Notice the healing energy this hug creates. Keep hugging as long as you like, and breathe deeply. Fill every cell of your body, mind, soul, and consciousness with this potent energy.

Know that with this imaginary hugging adventure, you give yourself exactly what energy you need. For example, if you choose a lion, you desire a shift to BE and live in your majestic power. If you choose a baby kitten, your desire is to BE and live in your gentle softness.

Plus this counts as an adventure, because you hug an animal which normally you can't. And the added energy of excitement an adventure carries, lifts the potency of this healing experience and brings a "wow" spark to your already-healing hug.

Hugs are healing! Hugs are "heart-energy" activating! Hugs are magical!

That IS happiness!

Day 125

Twirl your way to happiness!

Stand with your feet shoulder width apart, arms stretched out to your side, and fingers spread wide. Give it your flashiest smile and let's go!

Twirl to the right as fast or slow (because speed is not needed here), and as long as it is comfortable for you.

Then twirl to the left as fast or slow, and long as you like. If you get the urge to giggle, go for it—even better.

When ready, stop slowly and keep your arms stretched out. Breathe and feel this amazing shift that took place in your energetic space, mind, body, soul, and consciousness.

- You feel cleaner and lighter, because all your heavy stuff twirled off.
- You feel your personal energetic space bigger, because it is!
- You feel a stillness and pureness inside of you, because you detoxed.
- You feel free!

And do not underestimate all the fun, child-like playfulness you created in and for yourself.

Enjoy your twirling frequency!

That IS happiness!

Day 126

Imagine yourself taking a huge bite of your favorite food!

Close your eyes and taste, smell, hear, see, think, and feel this! Now voice your enjoyment with saying "Mmmmmmm..." while you eat this deliciousness! Really go all out and feel the yumminess while humming "Mmmmmm..." as long and loud as you would like.

Doing so shifts you to BE and live in your present "now-moment" of eating. That means you eat consciously, which is the only state in which you truly feel what and how much your body needs to eat or drink, in order to be healthy.

It also creates a delicious feeling for what you eat or drink at that moment, and food that you feel is delicious is food nourishing your body in a delicious way.

Not to mention all the smiles and giggles that you create for yourself and others when you are so outspoken about your enjoyment of eating and drinking.

"Mmmmmm..." shifts you to BE and live in a delicious high-for-life frequency.

Celebrate all "Mmmmm..." moments in your new day!

That IS happiness!

Day 127

Close your eyes, smile, and listen in stillness!

Listen to all this amazing life around you expressing itself through sounds and noises. What do you hear?

Move from sound to sound, and without judging, acknowledge it with "that is someone washing the dishes," "that is a child crying," "that is a bird singing," "that is a car alarm," or "that is a dog barking." This will fine-tune your ability to simply listen and hear everything that is there for you.

Now take this practice into your body, and listen in stillness to what every cell and organ is telling you. Acknowledge all sounds, noises, and information without judging. Simply hear all the incredible information your body has for you. That will fine-tune your ability to simply listen, hear, and understand what your body wants to tell you.

When you listen to the "what," skip the "why," and refrain from any judging, you shift to BE and live in a non-resistant frequency where all just is and allowed to be. There you can clearly hear what you are meant to understand and know.

That IS happiness!

Day 128

Imagine that you are a warrior!

You are strong, confident, and powerful. You are in charge and limitless in your capabilities, and you have infinite wisdom! Feel yourself in this!

Everyone has a personal warrior energy that feels good and fits for them. When you shift to BE and live in your warrior energy, you are and you live as that limitless power.

The easiest ways to shift is through:

- Meditation, wherein you connect to and feel your warrior.
- Visualization, in which you see yourself hiking up a mountain with super strength and once you conquered it, you stand tall and powerful on top, feeling your warrior.
- Exercising, in which you lift weights or practice strength training and feel your warrior.

You can also pick a warrior (famous, fictitious, or one in your neighborhood) that impresses you. Feel their warrior energy, because that lets you tune into your own warrior energy.

And last but not least start talking to your warrior!

Saying: "I am a warrior!" or "I am strong and powerful!" are great phrases to shift yourself to BE and live in your personal warrior frequency where you can conquer extraordinarily.

That IS happiness!

Day 129

Finding comfort is key!

When you find and feel comfort in what is happening for you, you shift to BE and live in a frequency of acceptance, respect, appreciation, gratitude, and love. And since all your happenings are meant for you to experience, you might as well get comfortable with all of them.

Comfort carries the energy of coziness, security, "all is OK," and "I am fine with what is." Saying the word "comfortable" to yourself and others, and feeling comfort shifts you to BE and live in all that goodness.

The happy happenings are easy to find comfort in. Enjoy, feel, see, hear, smell, taste, and think of them with joy.

The tough ones are the ones that are anything but happy. However, those are exactly the happenings you are gifted with to create comfort in, because they carry potent healing opportunities. Acknowledge them, and accept, respect, appreciate, thank, and love them as the gift they are for you, then create comfort in them.

For example, if you are unwell, create comfort in your *unwellness* with taking exceptional care of yourself with healing and loving self-talk, gentleness towards yourself and maybe some indulgence, like chocolate.

If you are in mourning, create comfort with honoring beautiful memories, practicing trust, and believing that you are supported and loved.

If you don't have enough money, create comfort with gratitude, feeling the ever-present abundance in and around you. That will shift your center of comfort to BE and live in an abundant frequency. From there, anything is possible.

Those steps release all resistance you have towards any happenings and without your resistance they can be fine happenings. Even if they don't feel comfortable at first.

Live in comfort!

That IS happiness!

Day 130

Imagine pouring your whole life through a colander, like with pasta that is done cooking.

What parts of your life would be the water going down the drain, and what parts would be your pasta to keep, eat, and digest?

Using the sifting qualities of a colander creates clarity in your life.

If you know instantly which parts are your water or pasta, you are good to go! Simply act on the clarity you received.

If not, you can make a list with two columns; one for pasta to keep, and one for water going down the drain. Take some time to regroup and fill those columns with happenings in your life.

Remember that all of the water parts did serve you once, just like the water served the pasta to cook perfectly, it is simply no longer needed. With gratitude, let it go down the drain.

As for the pasta, indulge, enjoy, and happy digesting!

This IS happiness!

Day 131

The gift of a visitor!

Think of a loved one calling you, saying "Hey, I have a few days off and I want to come visit. Is it beautiful where you live? What do you love about it, and why would it be an amazing place for me to visit, other than because you are there?"

You immediately jump on convincing that loved one to come visit you. You tell them about your beautiful home, all the breathtaking sights, the good food, and all the fun adventures and outings that are available.

When you rave about where and how you live, you refresh your feelings for all the goodness that is always there for you. It just became alive and vivid again.

So pretend you need to convince your loved one to come visit you. Pause and think about how you really feel; about where and how you live, what beauty there is for you, what you love about it, how happy you are there, and what new or old outings you love, or could enjoy.

Really indulge in these thoughts, visualizations and feelings. Be vivid and alive about them. Enjoy the shift to consciously see, hear, smell, taste, think, feel, and love where - and how - you live, again and again.

If by any chance you find that you are not happy where you live, you just clarified that a change is in order.

That IS happiness!

Day 132

Imagine yourself standing in front of a mirror!

See yourself and say:

"I accept, respect, appreciate, thank, and love myself completely and wholeheartedly; with all my ups and downs, my lefts and rights, and my forwards and backwards including my twists of anger, sadness, happiness, quirkiness, and uniqueness. I love all of me!" Feel these words!

If this feels hard for you at first, it is because of your old beliefs that you are not perfect, whole, or lovable. Since these old beliefs don't serve or feel good to you, ignore them and instead say the above as often as you can. Soon enough, they will become your new self-love habit, which shifts you to BE and live these words as your truth, because they are! Take it even further and say to yourself:

- I am fabulous!
- I am precious!
- I am beautiful and magnificent!

Go all out, talk amazing about yourself and to yourself, and never ever hold back!

Besides honoring yourself with this practice, you also release any resistance you have towards yourself, and without resistance you can enjoy this spectacular YOU, completely and wholeheartedly. You deserve it!

Don't forget to spread and share these healing words with others! They deserve them too.

That IS happiness!

Day 133

You, others, every word and sound, every smell and taste, every thought and feeling, and every happening are all vibrating energy. And vibrating means it is moving.

You can play with that movement!

For example, listen to music that moves and touches your heart. Close your eyes and instead of hearing the music, feel it as vibrations. Now take your hands and let them move freely with these vibrations. Up and down or side to side. Up with the higher and up-lifting vibrations, and down with the deeper, grounding vibrations. Let the music lead your hands. Enjoy this beautiful experience.

Here is an other example; if someone yells, instead of hearing the words and sounds, feel the heaviness and intensity of these low vibrations. Become aware of how they move and shift your energetic being. Now try to lighten and up-lift these vibrations by visualizing them wrapped in your love and light, once they leave the yelling person, and arriving at your being in a light, loving, happy vibrational state. Feel this!

Play with all the vibrations and experiment with them! It is all about practice!

That IS happiness!

Day 134

Your pain is your best friend! It never lies to you, it is straight up in your face, and it lets you know without hesitation that you are lost and not in your middle. It keeps you honest when you don't love yourself, and it is a great chit-chatter that loves to communicate and answer questions for you. It does all that because it loves you!

So behave towards your pain as you would towards your best friend:

- Acknowledge your pain. Say "I feel you!"
- Welcome it and tell it to stay as long as it needs to.
- Create space for your pain to be in, as you would for your best friend visiting.
- Accept, respect, appreciate, thank, and love your pain.
- You might even want to consider celebrating your amazing best friend.

When you fight your pain, you create resistance towards yourself, because your pain is a part of you. When you welcome it, you create a loving relationship with yourself and your pain, which makes for great team work.

Have a friendly chit-chat with your pain, and ask what your pain is here to teach and tell you. Ask what you need to do for yourself to heal your pain (not to make it go away). Then be responsible and follow your pain's instructions. Teamwork for the win!

That IS happiness!

Day 135

Imagine that you are running your own business.

Your business has many different employees who bring their best every day in order to make your company an abundance-filled experience. They show up, day by day, supercharged and ready.

In return, you show them acceptance, respect, appreciation, thankfulness, and love. You give them what they need, tell them how wonderful they are, and take exceptional care of them. Because you understand that keeping them happy, healthy, and loved, has them showing up with their superpowers every day.

That is a very well-run business, which makes it a high-for-life community!

Your physical body is your business!

You have many organs in your body, and they bring their best, every single day, in order to make life in your body an abundance-filled experience. They show up every day—super-charged and ready.

In return, you show them acceptance, respect, appreciation, thankfulness, and love. You give them what they need, tell them how wonderful they are, and take exceptional care of them. Because you understand that keeping them happy, healthy, and loved, keeps them showing up with their superpowers every day.

This is a very well-run body, which makes it a high-for-life community!

Agreed?

That IS happiness!

Day 136

Bless everything and everyone you feel you are having trouble with!

Doing so cleans your energy because it shifts you from your troubled feelings to BE and live in a state of love, acceptance, respect, appreciation, and gratitude. Which initiates the opportunity for you to let go and move on. And since all troubles are gifts in disguise, blessing them means you are blessing your gifts.

Let's start with blessing *what* already troubles you: Close your eyes and think of your troubles—either one by one or all of them together as a bundle. Acknowledge them without getting emotionally involved, and spend just enough time with them to bless them. Make your blessings short and sweet.

Next, bless *who* already troubles you: Close your eyes and consciously think about every person that troubles you—either one by one or all of them together as a package deal. Acknowledge them without getting involved, and make your blessings short, easy and simple.

Breathe. You are now reset, fresh, and ready to go! Moving forward in your new day, deal with all troubles straight away.

For example: If trouble shows up, acknowledge it without getting involved in - or judging - it. Immediately bless the trouble (which you know is a gift in disguise) with your well wishes. Feel how this instantly cleans and resets you, as it instantly cleans and resets your trouble as well. Because if you stop feeling it as a trouble, it can't be a trouble anymore. And that is a chance for dissolution!

That IS happiness!

Day 137

Imagine breathing in light that is in the color of your choice!

Make sure you choose one that shifts you to BE and live in your high-for-life frequency.

Breathing in, fill yourself to the brim with this colored, good feeling, healing light. Spread it and imagine every cell of your body, mind, soul, and consciousness becoming and being that light. Feel this!

Breathing out, let go of all *un-loving, un-fitting, un-happy* feelings, and thoughts that you have. Feel this!

If you like, imagine yourself waving them goodbye!

Then, breathe in your colored healing light again, fill yourself to the brim, and be that light. Repeat to breathe out all of the thoughts and beliefs you would like to let go of. Enjoy this until you feel squeaky clean!

Practice this healing cleansing method often in your new day, and feel your shift to BE and live energetically clean.

That IS happiness!

Day 138

Make some important decisions that will carry and support you throughout your new day.

Say or think "I decide to___!"

> BE my light and live in my light!
> BE my love and live in my love!
> BE my health and live in my health!
> BE my abundance and live in my abundance!
> BE my happiness and live in my happiness!
> BE my magic and live in my magic!

Make this list complete by adding any and all other decisions that are important for you.

By doing so you decide to BE and live in your truth, which shifts you to BE and live in your high-for-life frequency. And that is where all magnificence is!

These decisions are a day-changer, so rehearse them often!

That IS happiness!

Day 139

Pick something or someone you think very highly of!

It could be a family member, friend, historical figure, or something like the sky, moon, sun, or an animal.

Here comes the big question: Why do you think so highly of what you chose, and what qualities do you admire? Pause for a minute and make a mental list.

Now take your list and go through every single admiration. For example:

"I admire the pure peace and calm of what I chose." Feel that peace, and then say or think "I have that same quality, I admire that pure peace and calm in myself too." Take as much time as you need to go through your admiration list, feeling the beautiful shift taking place in you.

Admiration of others is a helpful tool to put the spotlight on what you are not seeing or feeling in yourself, because every single quality you admire you already have and already are.

So next time you find yourself thinking highly of someone, know that this is your time to discover and admire the same in you!

That IS happiness!

Day 140

Imagine you are standing at the gate of an incredible huge nature park. You are so excited to see, smell, taste, hear, think, and feel all of the plants, animals, birds, and scenery in there. You enter, and it is already breathtaking; you are in awe. You walk about 100 steps further into the park, then stop. You look to the left and to the right, and then turn around. You think, "That was great!" and then you leave out through the gate, back home.

You enjoyed what you experienced in that park fully and completely. Hey, it put you in awe! You filled your body, mind, soul, and consciousness with all that beauty - but there would have been so much more *amazing-ness* to experience. You did not receive everything that was there for you to indulge in, because you did not go deeper into that park.

Life is that park for you, and it offers you the opportunity to always experience everything fully and completely. Life also lets you be in charge, to make the choice of what you want to feel fully and completely, and what you would rather just feel for a little or not at all.

Knowing that, don't hold back! Enter deeply into all you want to experience, feel it fully and completely. And trust that you can always leave that experience from any point, if you want to.

As an example, when something or someone makes you smile, don't stop at the feeling of a little bit of smiling; enter this high-for-life smile, let it unfold and grow inside of you into a jump-for-joy smile. Experience and feel it fully and completely.

That IS happiness!

Day 141

Think of a radar speed sign blinking like crazy because you are driving too fast!

This sign is used as a traffic-calming device to slow you and everyone else down. When you see it blinking you check your speed and naturally slow down. With that, you become more aware of yourself and your doings; your car and everything around you. It shifts you into your now!

"Overwhelm" is your own personal radar speed sign. It is a life calming tool to slow you down and shift you into your now. When you feel overwhelmed, check your speed of living and slow down. Become aware of yourself, your doings, and everything around you.

It is also an invitation to look at what you are working on and how you are spending your time. When it is strongly non-fitting, it can seem that everything is going to fast. Either slow down, or if you can, make a change.

It can also be an indicator that you are too involved in feeling, living, and experiencing happenings that are not yours—which means they are not going at your perfect speed. If so, your involvement can be to support, help, be compassionate, and understanding towards the owner of the happening. Besides that, it is time to take your speed radar to heart, and let others' happenings race by like cars on the freeway.

Being overwhelmed keeps you from speeding!

That IS happiness!

Day 142

Imagine that you are meeting your NOW for a cup of tea and some chit-chat. Both of you are excited to catch up. You ask your NOW "How is it going?" Your NOW says, "It's going well." Your NOW asks, "How are you?" You say, "It could be better, my PAST keeps me busy with stuff that is too old for me, and my FUTURE keeps me busy with stuff that is too new right now." Your NOW says, "Well come live with me. I am always right here, which means I will keep you busy with stuff that is right now."

Go live in your NOW and observe yourself! If you are thinking about what was, you are closed off to your NOW. And if you are thinking about what will be, you are too occupied to be in your NOW.

Your NOW is all that you have, the best place to be, and the only time when you can make changes happen for you, which then create your next. Plus, your NOW represents new opportunities for new amazing experiences that are available for you. So ask yourself, how do I feel in my NOW? How do I react in my NOW? Through what beliefs am I experiencing my NOW? Am I in my high-for-life frequency right now? Then:

- Shift your physical body from not feeling good to feeling good by giving your body what it needs.
- Shift your mind with thinking positive thoughts. For example, from "I hate this" to "I love this."
- Shift your feelings and reactions from sadness to gratitude, and from anger to peace.

That IS happiness!

Day 143

Remember!

That word carries the energy of being grounded, rooted, and being pulled into your now and your truth.

Read and feel the following often in your new day:

- Remember that each day you wake up, you get the opportunity to make it the best new day ever!
- Remember that each day you show up to read this book, you nourish and cherish who you really are, right in your heart.
- Remember that each day you honor what you learn here, and act on the given wisdom, you honor yourself and grow.
- Remember that each day you decide to grow, you say "YES!" to widening and deepening your love for yourself.
- Remember that each day you say "YES!" to loving yourself, you live your truth of pure light and love.
- Remember during each moment, that you are an energetic being, meant to vibrate in a high-for-life frequency!

Please say you remember!

That IS happiness!

Day 144

Imagine a child, so super excited and "over the moon" happy that they squeeze their shoulders up and together, make little fists in front of their chest, pull their chin down a bit, smile, and shake with excitement.

Now remember you being that child! Visualize, relive, and re-feel your childhood moment when you felt that "over the moon" excitement and happiness. Feel it big and bigger, and fill yourself to the brim with it.

Or...

Stand in front of the mirror and watch yourself squeeze your shoulders together, make fists in front of your chest, pull your chin in, smile, and be that excited and happy. Say, "I am over the moon excited!" Feel it, build it up to big and bigger.

In your new day, practice being "over the moon" excited for no specific reason other than because you choose to feel that way. Shift yourself to your high-for-life frequency, without being attached to anything or anyone... which is the freest and purest way to be "over the moon" happy.

That IS happiness!

Day 145

Rejuvenating your energy is an important puzzle piece to be happy; just as eating clean food, sleeping a deep sleep, and exercising to stay fit is.

So let's rejuvenate your body, mind, soul, and consciousness with the following practice:

Imagine all the energetic impureness in you is being flushed downward through your whole body: starting at the crown, going down, and out through the bottom of your feet.

Then nourishing strength floods through the bottom of your feet and pulls upward all the way through your body, into your crown, and out of the top of your head.

Next imagine a healing and rejuvenating light (color it if you would like) entering your crown, filling every cell while flowing downward through your body, into your legs, and out of the bottom of your feet.

Repeat these visualizations until you feel rejuvenated, a happy and smiling way of being.

You can also practice these visualizations for others... if they are open and accepting. It will do wonders for them and you.

That IS happiness!

Day 146

"Come on and do the twist!"

Twists represent turns, bends, new ways, and initiate flexibility and a stretched presence. They are amazing catalysts to get something new jump-started, awakened, expanded, loosened, and changed. They help detox, flush out, and let go. Plus, they carry a playful and gentle energy.

So get twisting!

Twist your body with yoga, exercise, or dance, and feel the goodness that you create.

Twist your mind and thoughts. Imagine twisting them to the right, to experience different ways and thoughts. Let all visions and inspirations flow freely. Now twist them to the left, and experience how different and amazing it is there. Feel your mind and thoughts expanding and loosening up to new wisdom.

Twist your soul and consciousness. Imagine twisting your energetic being to the left, then to the right, up, and down. Let all new feelings and energies flow through you. Feel your energy expanding deep and wide.

Also notice all the twists around you: in bakery goods, candies, paintings, in crafting and clothing stores, and in nature. That will shift you to BE and live in all that twisty goodness too.

In your new day, twist things up and enjoy the enrichment of your new feelings, knowledge, understanding, wisdom, and ways, combined with the expansion of yourself.

That IS happiness!

Day 147

Think of a big house with a basement, first, second, third, fourth, fifth, and sixth floor. Every floor is one room, one window, and represents one phase of your life.

The basement is before birth. The first floor is your baby time. The second is your toddler phase. The third is your childhood. The fourth your teenage phase. The fifth is your young adult time, and the sixth floor is your NOW.

Every phase in your life carries experiences and feelings, which store themselves in the appropriate floor and room. Once there, you automatically feel through that phase of your life and see through that window.

Normally you live in your NOW phase, which means you are on your NOW floor, in your NOW room, looking through your NOW window, experiencing everything fresh and without any old feelings attached. But when something hurtful happens, it can easily get mixed up with old experiences and feelings. Which means you shift to an old floor, look through an old window, and feel through your old pain.

If you would have stayed on your NOW floor, it would probably not hurt (or at least not as much) because your old pain does not exist on your NOW floor.

When your feelings are hurt, ask "Is this hurting in my NOW, or did I change the floor?"

If you find that you have left your NOW, get back to it! I promise you it will be a different experience.

That IS happiness!

Day 148

Imagine you are making a delicious "life-smoothie" for your new day!

What feelings, colors, activities, foods, drinks, and energies do you put in?

- Love, fun, joy, happiness?
- Success, power, abundance?
- Peace, sweetness?
- Red, blue, yellow, green?
- Reading, a bubble bath, sauna, or exercise?
- Music, dancing?
- Meditation, rest and sleep?
- Water, tea, veggies, meat, bread, cheese, dessert?

Put all chosen ingredients in a blender. When mixed, imagine filling yourself with this perfect life-smoothie. Feel your shift to BE and live in your desired high-for-life frequency.

"Smoothie" also has more benefits... It carries the energy of soft, comfort, treat, sunshine, healthy, and happy. Playing around with the imagination of a smoothie shifts you to BE and live in that fun frequency.

This sets a wonderful tone for your new day, creates clarity, and initiates creativity. And if you act on all your chosen ingredients, you add immense happiness to your new day.

That IS happiness!

Day 149

Is it your perfect cup of coffee, or is it not?

Imagine you try a new coffee bean. You boil the water, grind the beans, and brew your coffee in a french press. It smells delicious, and you are so excited for it. But then comes the experience of tasting it: bitter is just the beginning of describing it. Not your cup of coffee for sure!

In order to find a fine solution, you have three high-for-life choices to choose from:

1. You drink it anyways without judging, and make the best of it.
2. You skip your morning coffee all together. No judging, just moving on.
3. You happily make a new pot with different beans that are perfect to your taste.

In number one, you make the best of what's happening with letting go of your expectations and find peace in how it is.

In number two, you leave what is happening behind and move on clean and clear.

In number three, you let go of what is and create something new, different, or better for you.

These three "good feeling" solutions are always there for you in any situation in your life. And the best thing is, they all will leave you clean and clear to move forward.

That IS happiness!

Day 150

Support your decisions!

Imagine a child looking at a bowl of candies and decides he wants to enjoy one. That decision sparks happiness and excitement in and for that child. He grabs the one that looks best, unwraps it, and pops it in his mouth. Deliciousness is created right then and there! The child smiles the whole time. Feel all the goodness in this happening!

A little later the child starts having a bellyache. Everyone says, "It's the candy, you should not have had that candy." That shifts the focus to what was, which can't be changed anymore. It adds guilt, which is the opposite of the happiness that was created in the first place. A better way is to support the earlier decision and treat the belly ache as a new and unrelated happening.

Always support your decisions, because at the time of your decision, you give your best to make a happy and fitting choice for you. Treat what comes next as new and unrelated, then decide new again and support again.

For example, you decide not to work out today. Support that decision. If you start second guessing, still support it, without judging or feeling guilty. Simply re-evaluate new and change to a more fitting decision. And go work out!

That IS happiness!

Day 151

Cultivating a pure heart is just as important as cultivating pure water.

If your water would be dirty and cloudy, you would filter it until it was clean, clear, and as pure as you can get it to be. Filter your heart with the same determination: until it is clean, clear, and as pure as you can get it to be!

An energetically dirty and cloudy heart hurts, is numb, and it cannot feel happiness or love very well. An energetically pure heart is healthy and feels love and happiness fully and strong.

Anything that shifts you to BE and live in your high-for-life frequency of happiness will be such a filter. When you feel good, you clean out the dust and dirt and make room for love.

So meditate, exercise, walk in nature, enjoy a nice cup of tea, laugh and play, watch a beautiful movie, listen to healing music, or hug and kiss. As long as it touches your heart you are golden, or should I say clean!

Then, live and feel in your heart, because just like filtered water, an unused heart will get stale. And you have to start filtering it all over again.

I promise that you will love living and feeling in your heart, because it means you are in alignment with who you really are. You live and feel though the most powerful frequency there is— love. And you see, hear, taste, smell, feel, think, and experience everything and everyone through your love lenses. So no matter what the happening is about, it will be hard for you to shift away from your happiness.

That IS happiness!

Day 152

Imagine a chef's kitchen at a five-star hotel.

Every single person working in that kitchen is playing an important part to make it a high-end restaurant. Together they succeed and co-create an outstanding place to dine.

We are all working in the same kitchen, cooking up life by having the power to co-create a high-end experience together. In every split second, we get to choose what we want to co-create with anyone and anything in our awareness.

Right now you are co-creating with this book, your family, job, car, food, and all that is there for you. So what are you co-creating?

Are you co-creating energy and joy with your food, by thinking energizing and joyful thoughts about it? Or are you co-creating weight gain and unease, because your thoughts are "That will make me fat and it's unhealthy?"

Are you co-creating love with people that are in a bad mood by showing compassion towards them, or are you co-creating anger by getting mad at their behavior?

Are you co-creating abundance with the weather by seeing the nourishment in the rain, or are you co-creating frustration, because you are frustrated at getting wet?

What you co-create effects everything and everyone, because everything is energy, connected, and shares its energies.

Choose happiness and love! That makes the world a better place, because we all are co-creating as ONE!

That IS happiness!

Day 153

Colors are a great tool to shift yourself to wellness!

Choose one that makes you feel amazing for your new day. For instance yellow. Then feel, think, hear, taste, smell, and see yourself being surrounded by it. Fill every cell of your being with the goodness of energies it carries. That shifts you to BE and live in a high-for-life frequency of yellow, or your chosen color.

Then enhance your wellness by:

- Choosing clothing in that color and feeling the color on your body!
- Choosing foods and drinks with that color and feeling the goodness entering and filling your body!
- Having your color present and ready on your phone or in a picture. Look at it and feel it often!

Also notice your chosen wellness color everywhere around you: in your home, at work, in stores, and in nature. In the case of yellow, see it on bananas, lemons, and in the sun. Pause when you see it! Re-feel and re-fill yourself with the high-for-life feelings you experienced by choosing your color earlier.

Colors are wellness, and colors are everywhere; which means wellness is everywhere.

That IS happiness!

Day 154

Imagine you create your garden for your new day.

You plant it with your thoughts, intentions, wishes, dreams, and your to-do list. Put all you have into your gardening skills and make it a spectacular garden for you to enjoy all day long.

If during your day, you catch yourself far away from your thoughts, intentions, wishes, dreams, and to-do list, know that you are not in your garden anymore. At some point you left and are either wandering around, or entered someone else's garden. And that someone filled their garden with their thoughts, intentions, wishes, dreams, and to-do list too.

Sometimes someone else's garden looks and feels amazing. If so, and with their consent, it is OK to visit their beautiful paradise, to sit down, put your feet up and hang out—maybe even take a nap. It is also OK to look around and find inspirations that you can copy into your garden. But there comes a time when it is right to say, "Thank you for having me", and return home to your paradise, because overstaying creates a disconnect with yourself.

If someone else's garden does not look or feel good, don't enter. Stay in your garden and talk to them over your fence. That way you stay true to yourself. If you already entered, acknowledge this and bow out with gratitude for what you have learned. Then leave to go back to your garden. If needed, race back home.

Being in your garden means that you can always garden, create, and rearrange it to fit you. You can plant new stuff and throw the old out. You are in charge in your paradise! And let's face it, your garden is the only one you could ever garden in anyways.

Create your dream paradise, and inspire others to do the same.

One garden at a time!

That IS happiness!

Day 155

Your NOW and your FORWARD go hand in hand!

Your NOW is where all your power lays. Your NOW is also where all the live-action is. It is the only time and place when you can create change actively, and since all future happenings rely on what is NOW, this is significant. So naturally your NOW is where you consciously want to be.

FORWARD is the way you want everything to go in order to grow, develop, and change. FORWARD is the way you want to see, hear, taste, smell, feel, and think while being in your NOW. Because if you know what your FORWARD should look like, you can make the appropriate forward changes in your NOW.

Being in your NOW while having an eye on your FORWARD creates a thriving next, and who doesn't wish for that?!

That IS happiness!

Day 156

Imagine you are at a store.

You are finished with what you came to get and decide it is time to leave. In other words, you are ready to move on, because where you are at is not fitting anymore. You pay, find the exit, step through it, and enter into the outside. By exiting, you let go or leave behind all that was in that store and move on into your new.

There is great healing in that happening. And the best part is, you are already a professionally trained "letting-goer!" because you practice this scenario all the time.

In your new day, use every time that you leave as a letting go tool. Simply choose all un-fitting happenings in your life, and consciously leave it behind whenever you step through a door out into your new.

Feel how freeing this practice is and get ready, because you might have nothing left to let go of, by the end of your day.

That IS happiness!

Day 157

When gentle becomes a healing opportunity! Everyone has their gentle side. Feeling your gentleness holds an enormous healing opportunity, because when you feel gentle, your heart opens big and wide. And such an open heart is capable of creating limitless love, and carry infinite self-healing and wisdom.

To feel it, look into the ever-so-healing mirror. See your gentleness in your kind eyes, pleasant smile, your soft skin, and your whole compassionate, kindhearted being. Breathe and feel this!

To initiate it, put on gentle clothing and shoes, and indulge in gentle foods and drinks. If unsure what that might be for you, ask "What is gentle for me today?"

To practice it, enjoy gentle exercise, meditation, a foam bath, listen to gentle music, or enjoy a gentle movie. Hang out with a furry friend and feel its gentleness, and surround yourself with gentle people in your new day.

To become aware of it, notice all gentleness around you: in people's faces and actions, gentle fabrics, colors and lights, in gentle scents, sounds and words.

Go have some fun, visit a high-end dessert store! Feel your shift to a frequency of gentleness just with looking at all the gently created sweet treats. Indulge in one, two, or three of them. With that fill yourself with the desert's gentleness, and with the gentleness of the artist who created them. All these ways of focusing on gentleness shifts you to BE and live in your high-for-life frequency of your gentleness. A truly healing space to be in!

That IS happiness!

Day 158

Your new day is like a spa with many opportunities to feel pampered!

Energizing and cleansing: Feel yourself oxygenating with every breath in - and cleansing the old non-fitting - with every breath out.

Hydrating and blessings: Feel yourself hydrating and moisturizing with the water you drink. Fill a glass of water and bless it with goodness. Time to drink that blessed water!

Refreshing and rejuvenating: Feel your body, mind, soul, and consciousness refreshing and rejuvenating while showering.

Color wellness: Surround yourself with colors. Indulge in feeling them, and fill every cell of your body, mind, soul, and consciousness with wellness. Color up, it feels amazing!

Relaxation: Surrender in hugs! Hugs open and activate your heart energy, shifting you to feeling loved.

Nourish and replenish: Indulge in delicious clean foods and drinks. Ask what you like, prepare with joy, and consciously devour them with a smile.

Spark happiness: Smile! When you lift the corners of your mouth into a smile, you lift your energy too.

Awaken and pamper: Give attention to your beautiful feet. Massage them, cream them, and walk barefoot. Notice the grounding foot massage in every barefoot step you take.

And not to forget, be perfumed: Go smell flowers or use essential oils, and feel yourself scented.

There is endless "spa magic" in your new day!

That IS happiness!

Day 159

To have an upward day, you have to live in an upward frequency!

Upward carries the energy of success, "elevated," "going up," and "higher and higher." Using upward as a word shifts you and anything or anyone you are calling upward to BE and live in an upward frequency.

Noticing all *upward-ness* gets you into that goodness too... think about when you get up from a chair: consciously felt, you will shift to an upward energy.

But there is more:

- Look up the stairs. Feel their upward-ness.
- Watch an upward flying plane. Feel its upward-ness.
- Play with an upward bouncing ball and feel the upward-ness.
- Enjoy an uplifting song, movie, or activity, and feel how you shift to BE and live in an upward frequency.

Upward is key!

That IS happiness!

Day 160

Visualize your beautiful light! Big, small, white, or colored. Make it fitting for you.

Say hello and welcome your light into your hands. Look at it and take your time to get to know each other. Imagine your light getting stronger and brighter, and bigger and taller. Picture it changing colors, being playful, dancing, and moving freely. Let your light show you how it is happiest. Play and have fun together!

When ready, move your light to your heart. Feel it entering your welcoming heart, filling every inch of you, from your feet to your crown. You become your luminous light. This shifts you to BE and live as the beaming light you really are!

The most powerful reaction to any non-fitting happening, is to focus on shining your light brighter and stronger than the non-fitting. So it is of utmost importance to feel, clean, nourish, and cherish your infinite bright light at all times. Practicing the above imagination will do that for you.

Shine strong, bright, and happy!

That IS happiness!

Day 161

There is a position open. Your life is looking for a leader. Interested?

Job description:

A fun, vivid, engaged job with lots of responsibilities and huge feel-good payback.

Must-have qualities to fill this job successfully:

You know you are in charge. You lead by moving forward with the purpose to feel good, and focus on happiness. You stay true to yourself, with that keeping your energy clean, pure, and free of gunk that is not yours. That clarity lets you share yourself confidently with everything and everyone around you, because you feel strong in your truth.
You are wide open to receive anything that comes into your awareness and understand that you have the power to choose what fits and what doesn't. You know with certainty that co-creating with what feeds your happiness is the way you want to experience this job. Your creativity is in overdrive, your energy is limitless, and your health is abundant.
You keep your heart wide open, and your love and light flowing with the job. You have trust in your leadership skills.

Does this sound like something you would like to do? I sure hope so. What are you waiting for? Take that leadership position in your life!

That IS happiness!

Day 162

Imagine you are at a ball, all dressy and fancy. You are smiling, dancing, and enjoying your wonderful time. A pure high-for-life experience.

But then, that one un-happy person who complains about the fruit plates not being fresh, the lights being too dim, and anything else they can find to complain about, arrives. Some of these complaints are valid, but some are not.

What will you do?

- Give up your happiness to join their un-happiness?
- Shift to *un-happiness* because of the true complaints, and maybe even join the complaining?

-OR-

- Stay in your happiness with focusing only on your high-for-life experience?

That scenario is given to you multiple times every single day.

Thinking about those questions and feeling what you would do gives you an awareness that prepares you for when they pop up. Reacting will be a piece of cake.

That IS happiness!

Day 163

Stop and look no further!

Magic is always right here: available and ready. You just have to to say "YES" to it and live it. You have to be open to see, hear, taste, smell, think, and feel it in everything and everyone.

Think about it: the amazing experience of life itself is magic. Your body, mind, soul, and consciousness are magic. You are magic!

And then there is magic in the sun, the moon and stars, the wind and rain, the snow, animals, the cities with all people, and the Earth and all beyond. It is all magic!

You are part of this magical, beautiful, possible, healthy, supported, happy, and peaceful place that is made of all this beautiful energy. That is magic!

Feel free to test what I am saying... Indulge into a piece of chocolate, and taste the magic!

In your new day, look at everything and everyone through your magic glasses. I promise you, you will be *magic-a-fied* in what you find, feel, and experience.

That IS happiness!

Day 164

Imagine a strawberry!

It is vibrantly red and definitely sticks out in a crowd of different fruits. It is sweet and creamy. Its texture is soft, and mixed with a crunchiness from the seeds. It carries a very vivid energy because of its color and taste, accompanied by fun from its seeds and shape. Imagining or really looking at a strawberry shifts you to BE and live in the high-for-life frequency of a strawberry.

Every fruit carries a certain energy you can use to shift yourself to BE and live in that certain frequency. All you have to do is pick your fitting fruit for your new day and ask the following:

- What feelings does this fruit represent for me?
- How do I feel looking at or imagining it?
- How does it taste when I bite into it?

Really feel your answers and let yourself shift to BE and live in that wonderful frequency of that fruit, and if you can, deliciously devour it. That adds vividness!

That IS happiness!

Day 165

What energy are you creating for yourself right now?

What you think, feel, see, hear, taste, and smell is all energy. Depending on its nature you fill every single cell of your body, mind, soul, and consciousness with either good feeling energy or not good feeling energy. Which then determines how you feel, good or not good.

Become aware of the quality of energies you create with asking yourself:

- What am I thinking right now?
- What am I feeling right now?
- What am I seeing right now?
- What am I hearing right now?
- What am I tasting right now?
- What am I smelling right now?

If you love what you are creating, keep creating. You are doing, and obviously feeling, wonderful!

If the energies don't feel good, make appropriate changes to the *what* and *how* you feel, see, hear, taste, smell, and think about things. For example, if you feel angry about someone, find something that you can love about them and focus on that. You shift from filling yourself with anger to filling up with love, and with that you will spread love.

That IS happiness!

Imagine that you are sitting somewhere and start tapping your feet to a beat.

Feel this happening!

Tapping carries the energy of happy, playful, fun, movement, and being energized. And your feet are your grounding partners that love to move, hence them walking you everywhere all day long. Putting those two in a working relationship together, you have a team that creates high-for-life energy in your whole being.

So tap away, either for real or in your imagination, and feel your shift to BE and live in a vivid frequency. Notice everything and everyone around you shifting with you. Soon enough, fun and smiles are created!

I say go and start that tapping movement!

That IS happiness!

Day 167

Chit-chat with what you find!

Everyone always finds something. Sometimes it's a leaf, a penny, feather, a piece of paper with a word or saying on it, or a piece of glitter. Stop when you do!

Pick it up if you can, look at it, and start some friendly chit-chat. Ask what it is there for, what it means for you, and what it wants to tell you. Then follow its guidance.

You will be surprised by all the information you get, which was meant for you to find.

For example:

I found a leaf in a funny spot on the kitchen floor. Funny, because it was not there at first but when I turned around, there it was. Since I was the only one at home, it rules out that someone in the family played a funny joke on me.

I picked it up, looked at it, and we started chit-chatting.

I came to find out that this leaf was my guide to keep me connected, grounded, and humble as the nature I am. It wanted me to take it everywhere I went in my new day. It gave me instructions to touch it often to feel its natural energy, simpleness, and pureness to keep me reminded; and that is what I did. I felt it as an amazing co-creation!

I hope you are now bursting with curiosity as to what you will find today!

That IS happiness!

Day 168

Become a programmer and program your breath to be a nutritious message for your whole being!

When you breathe in, think or say the first desire that comes to your mind. For example "Love." Breathe in and feel love filling every cell of your body, mind, soul, and consciousness. Then breathe out and empty yourself of everything that is not love. Wave it goodbye with gratitude.

Next, breathe in and think or say your next desire. For example, "Happiness." Feel happiness filling every cell of your being. Breathe out and empty yourself of everything that is not happiness. High-five it on its way out.

Then breathe in and think or say "Peace." Feel peace filling you. Breathe out and empty all that is not peace. Make a happy dance while watching it leave.

You are in charge of what energetic nutrition goes in and out of your door!

That IS happiness!

Day 169

When you decide to take a road trip, you choose a desired destination, plan the route, check the car, and the weather. You prepare and pack. Time to go!

You understand that the road conditions can change from curvy to straight or bumpy to smooth. Traffic can change from no traffic to a standstill, and so can the tempo from giving gas to hitting the breaks. A detour is always possible, and the weather and scenery can change constantly. You have absolute belief that everything can change at any second of your road trip.

And yet, you are confident, because you planned the route, accepted that change is normal and that you will adapt without problems. No matter what, you are excited and set on choosing to have fun!

Live your new day as an exciting road trip!

Set a desired destination of how and where you want to be at the end of your day. Plan the best route and attitude to get there. Pack and prepare so you set the right tone. Time to go!

Experience all with the understanding that the conditions of your day can change in every second, may even require a detour, hitting the brakes, or give more gas. That lets you be confident, because you planned and prepared, know that change is normal, and that you will adapt to anything without problems.

That is just how a day goes: it's an adventure! And no matter what, you are set to have fun.

Happy travels!

That IS happiness!

Day 170

Imagine yourself breathing and doing nothing! Weird, right?! But stay with me...

In this nothing time, you are actually doing everything. You are having a wonderful time with just being. Feel, see, taste, smell, hear, and think about all the space you create for high-for-life energies to enter and fill every cell of yours in that sacred time.

While doing nothing become aware of:

- The deep connection with your body, mind, soul, and consciousness you are creating.
- The self-love and self-healing that is taking place with you simply being.
- The wisdom, knowledge, understanding, and clarity you receive.
- The relaxation filling you, recharging you.
- The beauty and value that you can suddenly experience.
- Your huge happiness taking over every cell of your being.

Celebrate doing nothing, because through that, you celebrate doing everything!

That IS happiness!

Day 171

"You are amazing!" Not only are these words the truth for your whole being, they also carry an awesome energy of "breathtaking," "stunning," on top of the world, being powerful and incredible. Saying or thinking them shifts you, and whatever or whomever you call amazing, to BE and live in that high-for-life frequency. Try it! Say and feel:

- I am amazing! Feel your lips form a smile.
- You are amazing! Watch others light up with this sentence.
- This is amazing! Feel how pumped you get about what you are calling amazing.
- Life is amazing! Feel gratitude and excitement filling you.

If all you would do in your new day is sit at a street corner and call yourself, everything, and everyone amazing (no matter if true or not at the time), you would transform yourself, everything, and everyone to *amazing-ness*. And in a frequency of amazing, amazing things can happen. That is how powerful this sentence is.

So what are you waiting for?

There is also always amazing-ness presenting itself to you; in other people's actions, in nature, city life, or food. Notice, feel, and nourish yourself with this magnificence.

Be amazing, and get ready to find that your life is actually pretty amazing!

That IS happiness!

Day 172

Imagine that every time you open your hands, they fill with lots of confetti infused with high-for-life feelings you wish to spread. Once filled, you throw those pieces high up into the air. On their way back down they bless everything and everyone they encounter with the goodness of these infusions. Then they dissolve into Mother Earth, *nourishing* and *blessing* her too, sharing this goodness with the whole universe.

Every nice thought and feeling, smile, nice word, compliment, kindness, or help you give is one of those handfuls of confetti. It blesses whoever or whatever it encounters and nourishes the whole universe.

So throw your magical confetti generously, knowing that your shared high-for-life feelings and doings matter.

I call the imagination above a super-power imagination, because it creates super-power goodness.

Do you feel it?

That IS happiness!

Day 173

Joy, joyous, joyously, joyousness, joyful, joy-filled, jump for joy!

Are you feeling it yet?

The word joy carries the energy of happiness, bliss, fun, abundance, and bouncing *amazing-ness*. Saying, thinking, hearing, smelling, tasting, or seeing the word joy shifts you to BE and live in a jumping for joy frequency.

Saying to others, "You are pure joy!" gets them to bliss up with sparkling eyes, which they share with everything and everyone around them, including you.

So go and do what joy is for you; swing high on that swing, lick that yummy ice cream, or have that good laugh. Do whatever it takes, and enjoy watching the world around you turn to bliss!

Joy is always present. Take part in it, feel it, and fill up your joy tank.

Have a *joy-lishious* day today!

That IS happiness!

Day 174

Imagine having the power of super glue!

Super glue is some strong stuff. It carries the energy of force, strength, *forever-ness*, sticking, and connection. It also initiates trust in the person using it; trust that super glue will fix it, and hold it... forever!

Back to the super glue power:

I want you to glue yourself to your happiness - just like super glue sticks to your fingers when you are a messy *gluer*! It just won't come off anymore...

Then I want you to "feel" being glued to your happiness and indulge into the fact that no matter what is happening right now, or how strong the pull towards *un-happiness* is, you and your happiness are stuck with each other. I could not think of anything better to be stuck to.

Everything is always merely one option of experiencing. You have the power to choose what you want to stay glued to.

That IS happiness!

Day 175

Fierceness and power!

You might say, "These are some powerful qualities! But that is not me."

Well, that's not true. These qualities are energy just like everything else is. You are a cocktail made of all possible energies and are capable "as is" to feel your fierceness and power. You just have to become aware and consciously experience them.

May I present, your fierceness and power:

- The fierceness and power in every heart beat your strong heart produces.
- The fierce steps your powerful legs and feet take.
- The fierce and powerful moves your muscles handle.
- The fierce and power of every breath you take.

Focusing and feeling these examples shift you to BE and live in your frequency of fierceness and power.

Plus, using the words "fierce" and "power," or noticing all fierceness and power around you shifts you and all involved to that strong frequency too. And there is always the act of lifting weights, or watching a fierce hero movie that reminds you of your strength in you.

You ARE fierce and powerful!

That IS happiness!

Day 176

Imagine that you are standing in front of your brand new house. You are in awe. You get to live in this amazing place!

You walk to the front door, turn the key, and open the door. You put your hands on the door frame, say a blessing, then step inside. Wow, what a great feeling! You close the door and pause to look around.

It's all empty, clean, fresh, pure, and quiet. No one else's footprints, dirt, worries, anger, or negativity are present. It is you, your new house, and this wonderful emptiness, hanging out and having a sacred moment. You take a deep breath in this beautiful space of *nothing-ness*, dance in this pure emptiness, and enjoy feeling at peace.

In this imagination, you represent your mind, your new house is your physical body, and the emptiness is your energetic being; your soul and consciousness.

To experience the whole of you, you have to take your mind, go inside of your body, and hang out with your soul and consciousness. You have to breathe in your beautiful space of nothingness, dance in your pure emptiness, and enjoy feeling at peace. That will align you with who you really are.

From that state, you can then go outside and collect inspirations fitting for you, take them home and decorate your house, letting them add a fun touch to your already steady interior.

Enjoy your house and emptiness: play together, dance together, cry together, shine, and create a spectacular life together.

That IS happiness!

Day 177

Your TV remote control is a powerful device!

With it you can turn the TV on or off, change the channel, volume, color, and settings. Whoever has the remote shifts to being in charge. Which explains the high demand of people wanting it when watching something.

Now imagine you have a remote control for your life! That would put you in charge, no? So go, create a special one, make it any color and shape you like. Keep it small, so it fits in your pocket and is available whenever you need it.

You can:

- Use it for changing your channel. If you are stressed, change it to a relaxed frequency.
- Use it for changing the color. If you feel gray, change it to a colorful environment.
- Use it to change the volume. If life is too loud, change it to a quieter frequency.
- Use it to change any settings that are not fitting for you. Change your life to your preferred settings.

You are always just one click away from initiating change! Imagination is a powerful tool to get to the point!

That IS happiness!

Day 178

Imagine that there is this problem you have.

Picture yourself rejecting it and wanting it to go away.

Now picture yourself walking up close to it, hugging it, and say "I love you!" Maybe even "Glad you showed up, here is your lodging, stay as long as you need. Apologies that I can't stay and hang out, but I have got to go and live now." Out the door you go...

- Which reaction feels better?
- Which one is the high-for-life one?
- Which one is resistance free?
- And which one creates acceptance, respect, appreciation, and gratitude?

Embracing and loving your problems does not mean that you do not desire change. It simply means you accept and respect what is, shifting you to BE and live in a frequency where all change is allowed to be.

Addressing problems in that way shrinks them to be unimportant and small, and many times it dissolves them, because when there is no willingness to feel and indulge, there is no space for the problem to exist.

Embrace all happenings, just like life embraces you!

That IS happiness!

Day 179

Break the universal record of making yourself, everyone, and everything feel amazing about themselves!

When you uplift yourself and others, you all shift to BE and live in a high-for-life frequency. A fun state to be in and experience life.

You might be that one feel-good kick they need in order to get back on track with being happy. Think of how wonderful it is to be the one giving them that kick, and then get sprinkled with their happiness too.

As for the how, follow your inner guidance. You have all the knowing, understanding, and wisdom available in you. Serve, help, compliment, gift, admire, smile, hug, and be kind in any way. For example: if you see a child crying and throwing a tantrum, support the mom with a smile, a compliment, and kindness, then smile at the child and say something fun. That will make the mom feel better and the child might even break a giggle. It defuses the situation and initiates "feeling good" about each other. That is that kick I am talking about.

Be an up-lifter and make today a "feel spectacular" day for you and all!

Enjoy the ripple effect of that happiness!

That IS happiness!

Day 180

Imagine you and your loved ones are in a nice restaurant. You get served delicious food presented like art. You are excited and hungry, and you feel amazing and happy.

But then you notice a hair in your food! Yikes! You can't stop focusing on that hair and don't even notice the artful and delicious food anymore. Actually, you don't even have an appetite anymore. Even if they would bring you a new plate, you are done eating.

What happened?

Your focus shifted - then grew - and got so strong that you could not let go of it anymore.

In your new day, become aware of what you focus on and the shift you experience because of it!

Naturally, the best is to focus on staying in your happiness, but that is not always easy, is it? If you do lose grip, acknowledge your shift from happy to un-happy. Accept, respect, appreciate, thank, and love it for what it is: a great practice to get back to your happiness. Then shift, and enjoy being happy again.

It is all about your focus!

That IS happiness!

Day 181

Visualize and feel ahead!

Just like you plan ahead moment by moment or plan your schedule for the whole day, you can visualize and feel ahead moment by moment or your whole day.

The difference is, planning happens in your mind and creates what *needs* to be, which is not always a high-for-life way of being. Versus visualizing and feeling, that happens in your heart and creates how you *want* it to be, which is always a high-for-life way of being.

Add visualizing and feeling ahead to your planning, to create a great balance between what needs to be and how you want it.

For example, visualize and feel ahead:

- how you want to be in your new day.
- how you want to feel in your new day.
- how you want your new day to be.

Play with this! Make every visualization and "feel ahead" an exciting personal short film of your next moment or your new day.

You will be in awe of what you can manifest that way!

That IS happiness!

Day 182

Imagine that you have a love tank, a happiness tank, a nutrition tank, a sleep tank, a peace tank, etc.

These tanks hold your energy to experience a healthy, abundant, and amazing time in your physical life. They are also your juice to co-create with others and serve the world.

In a healthy and happy state these tanks are full and you feel great. But like a gas tank in a car, your tanks get used up by living your life. You have to make sure to re-fill them constantly, so they don't get low, leaving you not feeling good.

To re-fill, take exceptional care of yourself with self-love, nutrition, sleep, exercise, meditation, time in nature, laughter, play, and anything that makes you feel good and happy.

Living your life and serving the world while your tanks are low, runs you even lower. Which is not healthy nor a good way to live.

Living your life and serving the world while your tanks are filled, feels great and makes life a joy to live. And if you happen to have an overflow of your energies, you can serve the world with what you have too much of. Which is even better.

Re-fill those tanks, and let them overflow!

That IS happiness!

Day 183

Life is an ever changing and moving experience, and sometimes it changes faster than you can create differently.

So why even fuss about anything too much?

Why not give your un-happy happenings the time, space, and chance they need, to figure out if they can help or resolve themselves?

So try backing off - and acknowledge all of the happenings you are not happy about with an open heart. Smile! Release any resistance with saying or thinking "It is what it is! I accept, respect, appreciate, thank, and love it as is. It will all change anyways." Feel the relaxation this brings.

From there:

If you do have clarity about the change you would like and can create it right then and there, go for it! That is your momentum! Case solved!

If you are not clear or can't create a change right away, let it be as it is. Shift your focus on all happenings in your life that you love. Feel that joy! Once in a while check back in with the un-happy happening. Is it still there? Many times it will be resolved or simply not be such a big un-happy deal anymore.

That IS happiness!

Day 184

Imagine that you are going on a walk and notice a sign that reads, "Please keep this area clean!"

That right there is your heads-up to make sure to inform everyone in your awareness to keep your energetic space clean. It also serves as a reminder for you to get cleaning on your part with letting go of all non-fitting, and put an effort into staying clean!

Every little message and hint you notice is always meant for you as a personal gift of knowledge. Go ahead, have that important chit-chat with your heads-up alerts and get to the bottom of what you need to know!

That can go something like this:

"I see you! Thank you for showing up for me. What message do you have? What can you teach me? What do I need to know?" End with, "I accept, respect, appreciate, thank, and love the gift your are for me."

Taking what catches your eyes seriously lets you receive all that is there for you. And I mean ALL!

Heads-up in your new day!

That IS happiness!

Day 185

Start a high-for-life frequency journal!

Feel, hear, smell, taste, see, and think of everything in yourself that shifts you to BE and live in your high-for-life frequency. For example: your beautiful heart, your flowing water, your colorful blood, your happy feelings, your amazing eyes, your smile and laughter, and your energy.

Now think of everything and everyone around you that shifts you to BE and live in your high-for-life frequency. For example: your loved ones, your pets, your home, nature, the sun, and food.

Then go through activities, books, music, and anything that gets your heart jumping for joy.

Write all this incredible information in your high-for-life frequency journal.

If in your new day, you feel anything less that super and need a reminder of the what, how and who that makes you feel amazing, simply pull out your journal. It is all in writing; your clarity and truth of your happiness, your how-to create your happiness, and your road map to get to your happiness.

As your being and your life change, your what, how and who change too. Keep your journal fresh and updated with frequent changes and add-ons.

Happy *journaling*!

That IS happiness!

Day 186

Imagine that you are at the beach using a metal detector. You are scanning every inch of sand to find metal. Once you find something you dig it out and look at it with focus.

Scan your whole being the same way!

Start with your physical body; from your crown down to your feet, scan your body, first the front and then the back. Feel anything there is - pain, soreness, tightness, sadness, anger, jealousy, love, and joy. Refrain from judging and fixing anything. Simply feel and let it be.

Then scan your mind, scan your thoughts. Again, don't judge and don't fix. Just let them come and be.

Next, scan your soul; scan your energetic being. Feel your soul! No judging or fixing needed. Simply let it be.

And lastly, scan your consciousness, your now. How is your now? Don't judge and don't fix. Feel and let it be.

Becoming aware of all energies in your being means you acknowledge what is going on. It is the first step of being at peace with yourself. Refraining from judging and fixing anything means that all can - and is allowed to - be a wonderful message to your whole being that "Nothing is really wrong, all is OK!"

From there, solutions can arrive.

That IS happiness!

Day 187

What kind of water do you need right now?

Still for more inner stillness, or bubbles, for more bubbly energy?

Water is a spectacular delivery source of flowing, clean, moving, clear, detoxing, alive, and refreshing energy. Being mostly made of water means you are already all those energies. Add drinking plenty of water, or playing and hanging out in water, and you are left with no other choice than to BE and live in the wonderful frequency of water.

There is more...

If you add ingredients that match your energetic needs to water, you will create your own unique "water energy cocktail", that is filled with high-for-life energy; all customized to your needs. So ask yourself "What energy do I need?" and then add the fitting ingredients.

For example, add:

- Lemon for detox and a refresh.
- Honey for more inner sweetness.
- Fruit for fun and playfulness.
- Tea to fit your healing needs.
- Flower blooms for beauty and gentleness.

Mix and match consciously, and feel your "water energy cocktail" with its potent energies entering your body and fulfilling your needs.

That IS happiness!

Day 188

Imagine you are en-route on a road trip. At some point you stop to look where you are, and what time it is. You smile and say "Great! I am exactly where I am supposed to be."

Realizing and saying this feels good, because feeling OK with where you are at the time, creates acceptance, respect, appreciation, gratitude, and love for where you are and for what is happening right now. You are in peace.

Copy this exact way of seeing, thinking, hearing, smelling, tasting, and feeling into anything that is happening for you in your new day. Say to yourself often (especially when in doubt) "Great! I am exactly where I am supposed to be!" because it is the truth, you are exactly where you are supposed to be at this time!

Take it even further and say "I will make the best of everything that is happening right now, because what is, is just fine for me right now."

Feel your shift to peace with practicing this!

That IS happiness!

Day 189

Your beautiful mouth does a lot!

It does more than just show off your amazing lips, carry your powerful teeth, or be the gate for your wonderful voice to come to life through. Used properly, it can immediately lift and shift your energy into happiness through exercise and silliness.

Try it!

Start moving your mouth to the left, to the right, up and down, in and out, and make circles both ways. Get in front of a mirror if you can and try not to laugh!

Not only does your fabulous face get circulation going (and shifting you to flow because of it), it also energizes your whole being to feel fresh and young with lifting your energy. You create feelings of silliness and happiness, shifting you to joy. It makes you smile and laugh, and that is contagious for others.

Using your mouth in this way is an energy changer!

In your new day, consciously feel how you lift and shift to BE and live in a high-for-life frequency by having a playdate with your mouth.

That IS happiness!

Day 190

Imagine you are at a store buying a cookie.

You choose the cookie that looks best to you by believing it is delicious. You go home, excited to bite into it, because you believe it is delicious. Finally you sit at the table with a glass of milk, biting into your cookie, still believing it is delicious. And sure enough, it is delicious!

Your belief made it possible to create multiple delicious moments for you. All with a small belief in a cookie. Imagine what magnificence you can create with a big belief.

I urge you to believe:

- in yourself and your journey.
- that you are giving your best.
- that you are taken care of, loved, and guided.
- that you are deserving.
- that you are beautiful and healthy.
- in all of life and in your body, mind, soul, and consciousness.

Belief is a creation manufacturer—of love and happiness, new friendships, fun, and joy; new exciting work, art, music, and ideas; playfulness, smiles, and laughter; relaxation and peace.

Belief creates magic!

That IS happiness!

Day 191

ME for me, and only then with everyone together!

- I love ME, and only then, can I love everyone else.
- I make ME happy, and only then, can I be happy with others.
- I smile for ME, and only then, can I smile with everyone.
- I take care of ME, and only then, can I care for everyone else.
- I need ME, and only then, can I need others.

Fulfilling your ME tank on every level first, makes sure that what you share with others is amazing quality. It also guarantees that you know what it feels like to receive what you share, because you experienced it first hand. And it puts you in charge, because who else than yourself can really understand what you need, and then fulfill those needs in a perfect way?

Me for ME first! Say and think this to yourself often in your new day.

That IS happiness!

Day 192

Imagine that you are in your car listening to the radio and a person calls into the station, winning a trip to Paris. Wow! The caller's overjoyed reaction and the excitement created by the radio studio is absolutely spectacular. That powerful joy is energy, and it has the ability to overflow to each and everyone listening. YOU!

The question is, are you aware and open to feel it?

If the answer is yes, you automatically create your personal excitement for that winner, adding it on top of the already existing joy of the winner. Doubling the feel-good effect for you and the ones listening.

Every time you witness someone being excited you receive an opportunity to be lifted by their excitement, and can lift yourself even further with adding your own excitement for them.

The best part is that there are millions of reasons in every split second to be happy, overjoyed, and excited for others. For example:

- Someone making the subway train just in time before the door closes. Usually they are overjoyed.
- Someone forking in the last bite of a delicious chocolate cake. Usually they are happy as can be.

Use these moments to shoot like a rocket high up into their - and your - happiness. This goodness will be shared and spread, wider and wider.

That IS happiness!

Day 193

Remember when, as a child, you played on without end - happy and worry free - and how when it was time to stop playing, your frown and un-happiness were unleashed until you could play again?

You can be and live that playfully again, right here and right now!

Playful comes in many ways, shapes, and sizes:

- Walking in a playful way.
- Dressing in playful clothes.
- Eating playful food in a playful way.
- Speaking with playful words.
- Living your new day with a playful intent.
- Reacting to everything and everyone in a playful way.

When you are stressed, sad, or angry, pause and re-feel yourself as a child playing; happy and worry free. From there, you will be able to react to what is happening for you in a playful way.

Let yourself shift to BE and live in a playful frequency by noticing all playfulness in everything and everyone around you. If you have trouble shifting, watch children be and live playfully. That always helps!

In your new day, unleash the natural playfulness that is already present in every cell of your body, mind, soul, and consciousness.

That IS happiness!

Day 194

Picture a stopwatch!

You start it, you stop it, you reset it, and then have a fresh go.

Pretend you are using a stopwatch to reset yourself right now:

To stop: Right now for 2 minutes, stop moving and stand still. Stop seeing by closing your eyes. Stop hearing by covering your ears. Stop thinking, feeling, smelling, and tasting by focusing on your breath. Stop it all!

To reset: Uncover your ears and listen to all the noise around you. Acknowledge every sound by being in awe, and then letting it go.

Now open your eyes and see everything around you. Acknowledge everything with "Wow, that is beautiful!" then letting it go.

Focus on your thoughts with thinking, "I am beautiful, I am fabulous, I am smart, I am healthy." Make it fitting for you. And let it go.

To have a fresh go: Start wiggling everything, smile, and get moving again. Address every new step with "'This is the most amazing step ever." and keep moving.

Practice using a stop watch often in your new day, and feel reset and fresh all the time.

That IS happiness!

Day 195

Pick a person who inspires and really impresses you. Someone you think the world of.

If I ask you to tell me why you think so highly of them, you would reflect on their whole person, lives, happenings, and doings. You would list all they have accomplished and experienced and base your admiration on that.

I want you to do the same for yourself. Reflect on your whole being, life, happenings, and doings. Make a mental list of all you have accomplished and experienced so far and let loose with your admiration for yourself.

I know you will create a long, wonderful, and impressive list of all the many small, big to huge things you made possible and have experienced so far.

Your list will be magnificent. You will remember your *amaz-ing-ness*, and you will feel inspired, proud, and impressed by it all. Which means you will be amazed, inspired, impressed, and proud of yourself.

Celebrate yourself for what was, is, and yet to come for you; all made possible by *you*.

That IS happiness!

Day 196

Imagine that you are standing in a delicious ice cream parlor wanting ice cream really bad. But, there you are looking at your phone in search for an ice cream parlor out there. Sounds silly, right?

Searching for peace out there is just as silly!

You are already at peace, you *are* peace, and peace is already in you. Your being is the presence of peace. And since you are right here, peace is right here too. It is the most beautiful package deal ever, because you and peace are one!

Consciously become aware of your peace by pausing, breathing, closing your eyes, and tuning into your heart: the center of your peace. Say or think "I am peace!" and feel your peace! Stay there as long as you would like.

Once finished, move into your new day and be your peace.

Practice this often, and enjoy your shift to BE and live in a frequency of peace, where all peaceful happenings exist.

And just to be clear... ice cream is peace and peace is ice cream. So feel free to indulge in ice cream or anything else that means peace to you.

That IS happiness!

Day 197

Beautify your new day!

The word beautiful carries the energy of grace, charm, elegance, *stunning-ness*, pure, magical, special, and love. Saying or thinking the word "beautiful" opens your heart and shifts you, and who and what you call beautiful, to BE and live in a high-for-life frequency.

So add it to everything and everyone:

- My life is beautiful.
- This situation is beautiful.
- My job is beautiful.
- These people are beautiful.
- This tea is beautiful.

If this is hard for you or not true at this time, fake it until you feel it! I promise you it will come...

Indulge in noticing all beauty in and around you and enjoy other people's beauty with them!

Be that beautifier who beautifies everything and everyone! You got this!

That IS happiness!

Day 198

Imagine your perfect comfort zone! Nice, right? Feel how safe, comfortable, and relaxed you are while there. Feel how everything is known and familiar for you, in your wonderful comfort zone. When you are ready, I have question for you:

Are you totally or mostly living in your comfort zone?

If the answer is yes, you are not experiencing your life to the fullest because "new" and "different" do not lie in your comfort zone. New ways, views, opportunities, chances, ideas, feelings, healing, love, happiness, and "new" anything is always outside of your comfort zone.

I'm not saying you have to leave your comfort zone completely and go cold turkey, but rather leave it every day for as long as you can. More and more often, choose new and different over same old, same old. Go even further and choose what makes you nervous and uncomfortable over what already is comfortable.

Soon enough change, adventure, and excitement will take over your life. Things that you never dreamed of happening will be able to happen for you, because you are present in their frequency.

Your horizon will become infinite and you get to experience your "shine" in a way that you never knew was possible.

That IS happiness!

Day 199

Start an adventurous pact with your NOW!

Your NOW is always a guaranteed adventure because it is constantly new, updated, and filled with new opportunities for you.

Plus, you are in charge in your NOW, because you get to decide and choose your thoughts, feelings, and reactions; and with your choices, you create your next NOW. That is how - and where - change starts. Not to mention that you get to flash your super manifestation power in your NOW.

Your NOW is holding up its end of the deal: an adventure loaded with new happenings for you.

Are you holding up your end of the deal, to be present in your NOW?

Slow down often in your new day. Feel, see, smell, taste, hear, and think in a state of mindfulness. Make being present in your NOW who you are.

Magic happens in your mindful NOW!

That IS happiness!

Day 200

Imagine that you are taking a class, and that there is a vase of beautiful flowers next to the speaker.

You are mesmerized by them and can't stop looking; admiring and gushing about the flowers, the colors, and the energy they carry and spread to everyone - and everything - in the room. Feel this! This right there is an energy exchange!

It is of incredible healing value, because all of the qualities you admire in them, you have in you as well.

- All the beauty you see in them, you have too.
- All the colors in them, you have too.
- All the amazing energy they carry, you have too.

Pay attention and realize what qualities you admire in things, because everything that you think is striking, is a mirror for you to see and honor the same in you too. Feel, and shift to admire these qualities in yourself.

In your new day, experience every such exchange as the healing opportunity it is.

That IS happiness!

Day 201

You are always supported!

Support is an ongoing and constant happening. It is in and around you, and gifted to you all the time. Becoming aware of all support means that you shift to BE and live in a supported frequency - where you can feel safe and secure - letting your heart open wide. A supported being is able to rise to be the biggest supporter of itself, and has the strength to support everything and everyone else too.

Let's have a close look at all that support:

You are *supported* by your physical body, mind, soul, and consciousness to have an amazing experience in your life.

You are *supported* by your bed when you sleep, your car, subway, or bicycle when you travel, your shoes when you walk, and by chairs, benches, and sofas when you sit.

You are *supported* by the water and food giving you nutrition, hydration, and energy. You are supported by the sun, moon, and weather conditions giving you light, energy, and rest. And you are supported by all of the trees, giving you clean air.

You are *supported* by the universe. It always has your back!

As a support-feeling exercise, lean on a wall you like. Take a minute, breathe, and feel yourself being supported by this strong and secure wall. A wall is all about support, so it only makes sense if you take advantage of it and gift all the walls in your life with the opportunity to support you.

Feel supported and be a supporter!

That IS happiness!

Day 202

Imagine eating an orange that has no taste!

You would eat and get nutrition out of it, but not the pleasure of tasting it. That would make eating only half of the experience it is, right?

That would be like living your physical life, but not feeling it. It is only half of the experience, because your feelings are the messengers of your heart, and carry loads of pleasure.

So:

- Don't just wake up in the morning, feel yourself waking up.
- Don't just talk, feel what you say.
- Don't just think, feel your thoughts.
- Don't just taste and smell your food, feel it.
- Don't just hear or listen to music, feel the sounds.
- Don't just walk, feel yourself walking.
- Don't just see what comes into your awareness, feel it.

All of your feelings, regardless of what they are, are potent information and wisdom about and for you. Feeling them is the key to get to that wisdom!

In your new day, feel, and feel some more!

That IS happiness!

Day 203

Feeling good is a high-for-life frequency. It is where you want to BE.

Feeling not good is your personal wake-up call saying, "Hey, you are off track! Remember, you want to feel good, so do something about it." It is also your clarity tool, showing you without question what *does* feel good to you because without feeling badly, you would never know what feels good.

Acknowledge when you don't feel good. Accept, respect, appreciate, thank, and love it for showing up for you. That resolves any resistance you might have towards it. From there, ask yourself what changes you can make to shift yourself to BE and live in a good-feeling frequency.

But what if you don't feel good and can't create change right now? Find the part in your situation that does feels good. Given, sometimes it's so tiny you have to whip out a microscope, but it's always there, and you will find it.

Plus, there is always the opportunity to take charge and create a good feeling moment. Think how amazing a magical cup of tea, a delicious piece of chocolate, or a lip-smacking glass of wine is.

Do whatever it takes and be your own professional "feel good" creator!

That IS happiness!

Day 204

Imagine that you are having a blast while walking in a parade.

You see the mass of "all" standing on the sidewalk, waving and cheering at you. There is so much going on that, instead of seeing *all* the details, you catch glimpses of what and who is there. Some of these glimpses feel like fun, so you wave back wildly while flashing your biggest smile. Others don't feel so good; you acknowledge them and only respond with a minimal reaction. Since this is a moving parade, there's really no time for you to stop and dissect the "who and why" of the less than feel-good glimpses. So you simply move on.

Your new day is that parade, and - like in the example - you are walking in it. Everything is always waving and cheering at you as a mass. So you catch glimpses. It goes something like that: "Hey, look at me and join me being mad." "Hey, look over here and join me seeing beauty." "Hey, see me? Come and join me being kind." "Hey you, look at me and join me seeing everything as a bummer."

Now, which glimpses are you going to wildly wave back at and gift with your time and biggest smile, and which ones are you going to acknowledge with a minimal reaction and none of your time?

Your new day is a moving-on-and-forward kind of parade that simply does not give you time to stop and dissect what does not feel good. There is just too much goodness to see, hear, smell, taste, think, learn, and feel in every new step of your parade that you do not want to miss.

Have fun!

That IS happiness!

Day 205

Remember what is important!

- To feel good in your physical body, mind, soul, and consciousness.
- To listen deeply, follow your inner advice, and do good feeling things for your body.
- To acknowledge your mind, and shift to thinking good feeling thoughts.
- To be in your heart, the center of your soul, and live through your love.
- To consciously notice all good in your now, focus on that, and practice gratitude.

To practice feeling good with all your senses: See the good, smell the good, taste the good, hear the good, and feel the good in yourself, everything and everyone.

That shifts you to BE and live in a high-for-life frequency with every part of your whole being. Living your life becomes a joy! That goodness you go on and share with everyone and everything around you, making feeling good bigger and bigger, more and more, and spreading it wider and wider.

Remember, that is important!

That IS happiness!

Day 206

Imagine that you are vacationing at a new destination!

You feel amazing, are relaxed, trusting, peaceful, happy, and open to all new. You are breathing freely and deeply. You feel curious and adventurous. Food and water tastes better than ever. You have no rules for bedtime, meal time or a dress code and have no "to do-s." Life feels easy and is a piece of cake. You smile and laugh a lot. Your body, mind, soul, and consciousness clearly are in a high-for-life frequency. Feel this!

Your new day is just like one of these wonderful vacation days, because your new day is a new destination! You have never been in your new day before and you are clearly knowledgeable how to behave on vacation.

So:

- Be curious and adventurous.
- Breathe freely and deeply.
- Taste your food and water better than you ever have.
- Cancel all rules you can cancel.
- Feel life as easy and as a piece of cake.
- Be happy, smile, and laugh a lot.

If you must, feel free to put on your beach outfit to get your vacation feeling started!

Happy vacation today!

That IS happiness!

Day 207

Create a morning, mid-day, and night-time feel-good ritual!

Plan a few minutes during each time to honor, bless, and gratify your being and your existence.

For example:

When waking up, take a few minutes and feel your body, mind, soul, and consciousness and set your desired intention for your new creation play-day. Open up to all that is coming your way—all the blessings and gratitude for yourself, everyone, and everything!

Take a few minutes around mid-day to ground yourself. Feel your body, mind, soul, and consciousness. Release anything that has accumulated or resurfaced that is not serving you. Imagine letting it disappear into the air, then filling up with happiness and love, and blessings and gratitude for yourself, everyone, and everything!

Before you fall asleep, *de-clutter*, clean, and let go of any un-fitting leftovers from your day. Feel your whole being and imagine that you are filling every cell with light of your chosen color. Blessings and gratitude for yourself, everyone, and everything!

Make these rituals a priority in your new day and stick with them. Soon they'll become your sacred time that you cannot be without!

That IS happiness!

Day 208

Imagine that you are sitting on a comfy sofa, all relaxed and smiling. You are watching a fantastic 3D nature documentary. You feel, hear, taste, smell, think, and see all that is in this documentary very vividly—just as if you were there, but you are not!

That is because this documentary is energy, connected, and shares its energy with you.

If you feel amazing, you share your energy with everyone and everything, just like the documentary shared it with you. If you feel anything less than great, you share that as well. If others feel amazing or anything less than great, they share that too.

The good news is that everyone is in charge to choose what to shift to.

Think of all energies as always present and available in a buffet. You are in charge to decide which ones you want to experience. If you feel amazing, you don't have to shift to a lesser energy that others are sharing in this buffet; and if you are feeling less than great, you get to choose something fitting from the buffet.

In your new day, choose consciously what you would like to share, or to have shared with you.

That IS happiness!

Pick your favorite race car!

Imagine you are sitting in it and about to go drive this fabulous, powerful, and vivid car on a race car track. You are beyond excited to experience this to the fullest.

You start speeding up, but soon hit the brakes. You slow down and come to a stop again. So, here you are in this fabulous race car, blocked against fully experiencing this, all because of your old fears, anxieties, and feelings of not being capable or good enough. Your experience is less than satisfying.

Your old beliefs are the brakes in your life, and if you live them, you slow down and come to a stop. You can't do or experience what you are meant to—as this amazing human being in this magnificent adventure of life. These old brakes of yours keep you from having a fully satisfying experience.

So be conscious of them, notice when you hit them, become aware of how you feel once you stop, and ask yourself how you can speed up again.

This helps you to take your foot off those old brakes, go win this race, and hold up the trophy triumphantly at the end!

That IS happiness!

Day 210

Imagine that you are standing in front of a healing spa, about to go in.

You are looking forward to the relaxation, recharging, cleaning, and detoxing. You take a deep breath, open the door, and step in.

A spa carries the energy of pampering, healing, and gifting yourself with self-love. By taking the action of being excited for it, going to the spa, and actually stepping in, you already start to relax, detox, and clean—before even using the sauna or getting pampered.

Simply thinking and looking forward to going shifts you to BE and live in the feel-good frequency of a spa. The actual pampering in the spa is simply the cherry on the top.

In your new day, imagine that every door you enter is a spa door. Simply pause in front, imagine the spa entrance, set your spa intentions, and enjoy your shift to BE and live in your high-for-life spa frequency.

That IS happiness!

Day 211

"I think I'll just be happy today!"
    Sometimes it's that simple...

"I just choose to feel good, laugh and smile, dance and sing, and simply enjoy a fun time today, no matter what."

"I just choose to accept, respect, appreciate, thank, and love everything and everyone. I release any resistance I have towards anything or anyone. Resistance-free feels amazing!"

"I just choose to think, see, hear, feel, smell, and taste happiness in everything and everyone. Then I fill every cell of myself with this happiness, and go on to create more of this highf-or-life feeling."

And if someone asks what happened to me, I say "Well, I started my new day by thinking, 'I'll just be happy today!'"
    Practice this simpleness! It works every time.

That IS happiness!

Day 212

Your focus!

To work with your focus, you have to locate it first. Ask, "Where is my focus, on me, or out there on others?" If it's on you, great job! Keep it up! If it's out there, maybe even on others, pull it into and onto yourself. Feel your focus on yourself and imagine it strong and disciplined!

Challenge yourself by asking:

- How strongly can I focus on my peace and happiness inside of me?
- How strongly can I focus on all abundance?
- How strongly can I focus on being healthy?
- How strongly can I focus on all that is going right for me, and the good in everything and everyone?

Use your powerful focus to create change for yourself. Acknowledge - but don't get emotionally entangled in - all happenings that are not as you wish. Ask, "How do I want them to be?" then focus with strength and discipline on the desired outcome, and enjoy the change you are creating.

If you find yourself slipping back to focusing on others or the unwanted outcome, simply acknowledge it and shift back to you and your wanted outcome. And stick to it like super glue.

That IS happiness!

Day 213

Imagine that you are driving by a beautiful meadow filled with different wild flowers, grass, and weeds all mixed together.

The view and how it makes you feel shifts you and your new day to BE and live in the frequency of that beauty. The next day you drive by that meadow, the traffic light changes to red and you have to stop. This creates a little time for you to look at it all, close up and in more detail. You see that there are also lots of dead and *un-pretty* growth in between all these beautiful wild flowers. Focusing on the un-pretty gives you a completely different feeling than last time when all you saw was the beauty. It's clearly not as good of a feeling.

Right then and there, you have a choice:

Do you keep seeing the beautiful meadow as a whole and focus on how amazing this magical sight makes you feel? Or do you now only see the un-pretty and focus on the less-than-amazing feeling you have shifted to?

Everything always has multiple sides! Multiple sides to see, hear, taste, smell, feel, and think of. Naturally, one side always feels better than the others. That clears up any questions you might have about what side to focus on: always choose the best feeling one.

Even though I advise you to focus on the better feeling one, it is absolutely necessary to acknowledge, accept, respect, appreciate, thank, and love all sides that exist, because the full experience is a gift.

That IS happiness!

Day 214

Go smell all of the deliciousness!

Delicious smells carry delicious energy and initiate delicious feelings in and for you; like feeling fresh, relaxed, energized, luxurious, sweet, loved, and abundant. Smelling and feeling deliciousness shifts you to BE and live in a high-for-life frequency—which naturally makes for a delicious day!

Some delicious smelling - and feeling - opportunities are:

- Walk in nature and smell all of the plants, trees, flowers, dirt, and the water.
- Stick your nose high into the sky and smell the air.
- Walk on the beach and smell the sand, salt, and the sea.
- Go to a store and smell all the organic essential oils they have.
- Step into a bakery and smell all of the yummy baked goods.
- Stick your nose into a fabulous restaurant and take a big delicious whiff.

Smell and feel whatever fits your range of delicious in your new day!

Go all *delish*!

That IS happiness!

Day 215

Imagine a squeaky-clean floor!

See how clean and shiny it is, how clear and fresh it feels, and how light its energy is.

You can be in a state of that cleanliness, freshness, and lightness with your thoughts and feelings too! Here is how:

Notice all your "non-fitting" thoughts and feelings—you know, the ones that don't make you feel like a superstar—that show up for you. Acknowledge them one by one without getting emotionally invested or judging them. Then, have a cleansing chit-chat with them. Tell them you accept, respect, appreciate, thank, and love them, for the clarity creating tool they are for you—but that it is time for you to move on, and for them to move out. Tell them they are free to go, then move on, and shift to a better feeling and thought that fits you. Breathe and feel your shift to BE and live in frequency of squeaky clean thoughts and feelings.

Happy cleaning in your new day!

That IS happiness!

Day 216

Being open is a receiving way of being!

"Open" carries the energy of welcoming anything. Saying or thinking "I am open for all that IS and all that will BE for me!" shifts you to BE and live in an open frequency. Noticing all *open-ness* around you, in the actions of other people, in doors, and objects that are open, shifts you to that welcoming goodness too.

Being open means that you let go of all resistance, control, and expectations. This keeps your energetic being clean and able to receive all happenings coming your way freely.

It means that you create peace and quiet for yourself, so you can connect and hear what is there for you to hear; allowing all understanding, knowledge, and wisdom to arrive freely, and make transitions and changes good for you.

Being open means that you diffuse difficult situations by seeing all happenings as a gift, and remove the urge to always have to understand the why and the what.

It means that you create harmony in yourself, and accept, respect, appreciate, thank, and love all that is happening for you.

That makes for an open day!

That IS happiness!

Day 217

Imagine that every time you have hope, you send a magical balloon filled with positivity, *uplift-tivity*, betterment, intention, compassion, love, and support up into the universe. And once up high, your hope balloon pops, showering everything and everyone with all the goodness you created.

Now make it personal. Close your eyes and say or think "I hope...!" Fill in the blanks with your most desired hope. Then imagine your balloon soaring up high, popping, and showering everyone and everything with the energy of your hope, shifting you to BE and live in the frequency of your hope.

You can also create hope for others. Just remember, the only right way to use that power is with their wishes and "want" as the highest priority in the hope that you send out for them.

A day of hope is a day filled with magic!

That IS happiness!

Day 218

All those little messages and signs!

This is a reminder for you to really hear, see, smell, taste, think, and feel all these little messages and signs that are given to you in every split second of your new day. They are exactly what you need, to shift to BE and live in your high-for-life frequency.

Here is my little story to explain:

I am at the UPS store dropping off a package. All business is done. I ask "Am I good?" The answer I got was, "You are always good!" That made me stop, and every cell of mine filled up with that powerful message. I replied "Yes, I am always good, and so are you! Thank you!" Smiles and gratitude were exchanged. I left UPS a package lighter and super charged with the powerful energy of knowing and feeling that "I am always good".

I urge you to pay attention and notice all these little messages and signs that try to make your new day one-of-a-kind and shift you to BE and live in your high-for-life frequency.

That IS happiness!

Day 219

Imagine that you are lighting a candle while talking to someone and thinking about work. Once the candle is lit, you look at it for a second thinking, "That's pretty!" and then you go make dinner.

Versus:

You are lighting a candle consciously and you're present with the match, the candle, and its flame. Your thoughts and feelings are aware of your hands holding the match, your eyes seeing the candle, your nose smelling the burning scent, and your ears hearing the sizzling of the match. Once the candle is lit, you sit and stay with it, the same way the candle stays with you. You two spend quality time together. You watch its flame and start chatting with it about life. You have some really good laughs together. You realize that at this moment you, this candle, and its flame are all you were ever searching for, and you have all the answers, understanding, wisdom, and peace you ever wished for. You know and feel that right now, life is this candle and its flame.

Life is whatever you are doing right now and whatever or whomever you are with at this moment; be it brewing tea, making a meal, cleaning your house, working, driving, spending time with people, taking a shower, grocery shopping, or finding a rock. These are all parts of life, and all you will ever need to be happy at that moment.

What IS right now contains everything for you. So be conscious!

That IS happiness!

Day 220

Have you ever needed to go somewhere and do something that every cell in you simply did not agree with?

Of course, we all have!

The best and least exhausting recipe to get through that, is to BE and live in your happy high-for-life frequency before you start it, and then while you do it.

So commit to:

- Be tickled pink with your happiness!
- Be elatedly positive!
- Be euphorically smiling!
- Be blissfully yourself!
- Be joyously perky!
- Be jubilantly nice!
- And be delightedly giddy to get through anything that does not agree with you and can't be changed right now.

You will have a blast, everyone with you will have a blast, and your time will fly as a blast. Most of all, you will feel great afterwards. You will be filled with happiness and new fun experiences, overriding your old, un-fitting, and dusty ones.

In your new day, commit to be your happy you!

That IS happiness!

Day 221

Imagine that your first thought waking up, and your last thought falling asleep, is "I am grateful!"

Feel the beautiful tone you've set for your new day and your sleep.

Gratefulness and the word "grateful" carry the energy of *enough-ness*, *plenty-ness*, love, peacefulness, contentment, and relaxation. Saying, thinking, and practicing gratefulness shifts you to BE and live in a high-for-life frequency. That state is where your heart can open wide, and love can be felt.

In your new day, say and think "I am grateful...!" often. Fill in the blanks with what is happening. That shifts you and your NOW to "All is fine!" And it overrides any un-happiness you experience.

Tell everyone and everything around you how grateful you are for them. Feel hearts being opened and watch them fill with love.

Notice all gratefulness felt by others. Join in, and feel grateful with them.

Make being a gratefulness creator, spreader, instigator, and *inspirer* a priority for you!

That IS happiness!

Day 222

Remember a time when you were "over the moon" happy!

Re-live and re-watch that moment like a movie, and re-feel the "over the moon" happiness you felt back then. Dwell in it! Doing this re-creates your high-for-life feeling, which means you shift to BE and live in that frequency again. And it reminds you that you are already a trained and experienced happiness feeler!

You will also shift everyone and everything to BE and live in their own happiness, because nobody that is open and receiving can stay in a low frequency if you are "over the moon" happy.

Bring all your great memories and feelings back to life! They are yours to use. Utilize them as a tool to shift from unhappy to happy with re-thinking, re-living, and re-feeling them.

Have a great time while you are at it, then move forward in your new day and create more new ones just like them!

That IS happiness!

Day 223

Imagine you are on a beautiful island!

Sandy beach, happy palm trees, turquoise water, clear blue sky, and the sun shining. You are napping in a hammock under palm trees and begin to wake. You open your eyes and all you can see, hear, smell, taste, think, and feel is the absolute beauty of your surroundings. You are in awe! The vision fills your mind, body, soul, and consciousness to the brim with happiness. You smile! All is well.

After a while, you also notice the chipped paint on the bungalow, the algae on the beach, the smell of trash, and the holes in the hammock; and yet, all of this does not matter a bit to you, and are tiny compared to this gigantic beauty you saw, and focused on first, when opening your eyes.

Train yourself to see, hear, smell, taste, think, and feel, the gigantic beauty of everything and everyone first, and focus on that. Shift to BE and live in a frequency of *amazing-ness*, and anything less will become tiny and unimportant.

In short... Just see the beach, water, palm trees, sky, and sun in everything first!

That IS happiness!

Day 224

Here is why you should go bake your own cake:

Imagine someone close to you bakes their own cake, designed to their preference and deliciousness. They finished making it, but arc not necessarily showing or offering the cake to you. It is simply there, and you see their finished yummy cake. You can't resist, so you stick your finger in, take a nice bite, and start licking. "Wow, that tastes so good..." when you then realize that they never offered it to you, and this is not your cake to taste. Oops!

Now imagine this story if you had your own personalized cake made and finished. It would be very different. You could walk up, show your cake, and suggest a taste exchange. Not only would this be a delicious tasting experience, but also a fair and pure exchange.

That goes the same with happiness. If someone creates their own happiness and you would love to be part of it, it is best if you create your own happiness first, and then suggest a happiness exchange.

So, are you an accomplished happiness maker? Or would it be urgently needed for you to go and make your own amazing happiness first?

Enjoy making, exchanging, and tasting!

That IS happiness!

Day 225

Imagine a sky with lots of colorful balloons to take all your worries!

Worries create energy that shift you in the total opposite direction of your happiness, abundance, and health. They are usually about things that have not happened, or might not even happen at all. Which means you invest energy into what might be, instead of investing it into living right now. By giving them all your focus, you can't manifest what you want.

When a worry shows up, acknowledge it without feeling it. Say or think "I accept, respect, appreciate, thank, and love you." That resolves any resistance you have towards your worry, and it insures that no new ones are created.

Then, imagine you pick a balloon you like, and pull it down close. Write your worry on the tag on the balloon, bless it, and let the balloon - together with your worry - fly high up into the sky. Watch them with a smile and with gratitude until you can't see them anymore, transforming your worry into a beautiful goodbye sight.

Love your worries, let them be beautiful by flying high into the sky, and trust that all is well.

That IS happiness!

Day 226

Find comfort in the uncomfortable!

Life is an ever changing, shifting, and vibrantly alive experience. You as a whole - your body, mind, soul, and consciousness - are an ever-changing, shifting, and vibrantly alive being. Everything and everyone else is too. That is the natural state of all there is.

The key is to get comfortable in this uncomfortable, unknowing, ever changing, and shifting state, but why is that so hard?

Fear is usually the culprit! To feel safe, we find comfort in everything being settled and staying as it is. At first, that feels good and seems like a comfortable state. But soon enough it does not feel good anymore because it resists the natural state of everything being ever-changing. And change always arrives at some point!

First... Trust! Trust neutralizes fear. "I trust that..." Fill in the blanks and feel how your fear cannot exist when you trust.

Then... Believe! "I believe that..." Fill in the blanks and feel how you shift to BE and live in a comfortable frequency. Believing seals the deal to feeling comfortable in whatever is happening for your right now.

Be comfortable in your crazy alive state of discomfort!

That IS happiness!

Day 227

Imagine a day where you and everyone else expects that all is well.

Feel the tone of wellness that is set with this!

"All is well" carries the energy of good, "perfect as-is," and "worry-free" no matter what.

Saying or thinking "All is well" shifts you to BE and live in that high-for-life frequency. Saying "All is well" towards others shifts them to BE and live there too. Together, as this "All is well" feeling team, you share this goodness with everything and everyone.

In your new day, practice expecting that:

- All people in my awareness are well-meaning and are well.
- All situations and happenings are well-meaning and are well.
- My car, my home, my job, my bank account, and my bills mean well and are well.
- Everything that happened in my past meant well.
- Everything that is in my now means well and is well.
- Everything in my future will mean well.

Then be prepared for a pretty well day! Enjoy!

That IS happiness!

Day 228

Stand proud and make it happen!

Waiting for everyone to understand what you want and the way you want it, while treating you as you want to be treated, is a real gamble - and it may not even work or happen. But you are giving your power away, and regardless the outcome, your experience will be very muted because it was not you who made it all happen.

So:

- Make yourself visible, heard, outspoken, felt, and thought of!
- Make space, take charge, and stand up for what you want!
- Go create and take what you dream of!
- Be the most powerful advocate for yourself and what you wish for!

Go make it all happen in your new day!

That IS happiness!

Day 229

Picture how lava spreads and flows wider and wider, and farther and farther.

Now imagine yourself as a whole: your body, mind, soul, and consciousness, stretching like that lava, wider and wider, and farther and father. In that process, your being will cover a wider territory going beyond what is already normal for you.

Think of all the happenings that don't feel good, you don't agree with, or don't understand. These uncomfortable places are where you should spread yourself wider and wider, and farther and farther. That will let you cover a wider territory of solutions, teachings, understanding, knowledge, and wisdom. Learn to see, hear, smell, taste, feel, and think about all your happenings in new ways.

Spread yourself wider, grow wiser and grander, and gain new ways of being you.

That IS happiness!

Day 230

How do you pour your coffee or tea?

I am going to take a real safe guess here, and say that you pour it very determinedly into a cup, instead of kind-of-sort-of point the stream of coffee or tea at the cup and loosely hit or miss. Some of you might even go all out and choose a cup you really like, or have a ritual for pouring your tea into a very nice cup. Either way, your focus is on pouring into the cup without spilling or wasting it.

I invite you to do the same with your energy, love, compassion, and your light.

Focus yourself to pour your energy without spilling or wasting!

The cup can be yourself, someone, or something else, or even better, choose many someones and somethings you really love, are passionate about, and feel good to you. Then - very precisely - start to pour your energy, love, compassion, and light into it. Enjoy the goodness you co-create with that someone or something.

Fill it and don't spill it!

That IS happiness!

Day 231

Imagine that you are in a swimming pool!

You don't move against the water like it's your biggest enemy, because it would get you nowhere, exhaust you, and keep you from having fun. Instead, you relax and find a harmonious rhythm to swim and float with the water. You become one with the water. A wonderful feeling!

The water in the pool represents your life. Moving against your life will get you nowhere, exhaust you, and definitely is not fun, but relaxing and finding a harmonious rhythm to swim in - and float with - your life, no matter what is happening for you, will feel wonderful.

When your life does not feel good, is exhausting, or is no fun, you are moving against your life! Acknowledge it. Accept, respect, appreciate, thank, and love it. Then, close your eyes and imagine yourself sliding or submerging into a pool of water. Feel yourself relaxing and moving with it in a harmonious rhythm. Now, switch the water with your life, and feel yourself moving harmoniously with your life. This will shift you to BE and live in your high-for-life frequency where you can plan your next swim.

Move WITH your life, together as ONE!

That IS happiness!

Day 232

"But why?"

That is a popular and very delicate question.

On one hand, it brings you further when things are not working out. You ask "why" to find out the what, so that you can change the it. A wonderful way to shift yourself from un-happy to happy, deep into your heart.

On the other hand, asking "But why?" when you have an inspiration, idea, wish, or dream, will automatically stop your flow or momentum for that amazing thought. You shift from happily living in your heart to "I have to understand the why" which brings us into a sticky mess.

Choose your "But why?" moments wisely:

If you are un-happy, ask the why so that you can shift to being happy.

If you are happy, don't mind the why.

That IS happiness!

Day 233

Imagine that there is a trampoline for every possible feeling you experience.

Once you have a feeling, you are automatically jumping on that trampoline. For example: If you feel love, you are jumping on the love trampoline, refilling with more love every jump you take, and only love manifestations exist on that trampoline.

This also means that if you are angry then you are immediately jumping on the angry trampoline, keeping yourself refilled with renewed anger, and only angry manifestations exist there.

The goal is to mostly jump on trampolines that are made of high-for-life frequencies like happiness, love, excitement, abundance, playfulness, and healthiness. But even if you find yourself angry, that is OK! Acknowledge it, accept, respect, appreciate, thank, and love your anger for the powerful energy it is for you. If you would like, keep jumping a bit on your angry trampoline until it feels good to leave. Then, when you're done, shift your feeling to a high-for-life frequency and find yourself jumping on a feel-good trampoline—refueling and manifesting amazing things in no time!

Happy jumping!

That IS happiness!

Day 234

Imagine a giraffe!

Picture this, the tallest animal in the world, and focus on its long, high neck. Admire it as long as you like.

When ready, visualize yourself slipping in, and being that giraffe. Then through the giraffe's eyes, look around you in that high-altitude space. Feel how it is for you: to be that tall animal and to see everything through that height.

With this imagination, you experience the energy of a giraffe, which means you shift to BE and live in the frequency of tallness and *longness*!

That can feel something like this:

- The air and energy is clear, clean, and open, high up here.
- It is beautiful to be able to overlook everything.
- The view, the thoughts, and the feelings are pure, because it is only you and the sky.
- Creative thoughts come easy in this clear space up here.
- You connect deeply and feel yourself crystal clear in this height.

Play with and practice this imagination often in your new day and enjoy the high-for-life frequency of clarity while you are high in the sky.

It's fun to be a giraffe!

That IS happiness!

Day 235

Imagine that you are opening your eyes to your new day of happiness.

All you can see, hear, taste, smell, feel, and think of is happiness in you, everyone, and everything. Feel this high-for-life tone you are setting for your new day!

Happiness carries the energy of joy, wonderfulness, magnificence, health, aliveness, vividness, and smiles. Focusing on happiness in and around you shifts you to BE and live in that great frequency. You will fill every cell of your body, mind, soul and consciousness with this goodness, and go on sharing it with everyone and everything around you.

So:

- Notice all of the happiness in every breath you take.
- Notice all of the happiness in you and others.
- Notice all of the happiness in your food and drinks.
- Notice all of the happiness in the air.
- Notice all of the happiness in colors and sounds.

Set your intention to focus on all of it!

That IS happiness!

Day 236

Enjoy all your winner moments!

How many times a day do you feel like an amazing winner, but don't notice it, take it as normal, get caught up in the why, or talk yourself out of it, even though you feel it and it is yours to celebrate?

Here is my little story as an example:

I was overcome by this amazing feeling that I won big time, because I made it through an "orange" traffic light (you know the one... it is not quite red yet, but it certainly isn't still yellow!) that usually takes forever to turn green again. So here I was, driving down the road, smiling and filled with this amazing high-for-life feeling of winning. I indulged into this goodness, and then went on to acknowledge everything and everyone as a winner for the rest of my new day. It went something like this:

- I just made another green light; I am a winner!
- I got my daughter to campus on time; we are both winners!
- We enjoy where we live; my whole family is winning!

For me it was this traffic light. For you, it might be catching the subway train, buying the last loaf of bread in the store, or simply just feeling like a winner because you enjoy where you live.

In your new day, notice all your winner moments and indulge in them!

That IS happiness!

Day 237

Imagine yourself sitting on a swing.

You start swinging. At first, you swing slow and low, back and forth. Then your swinging gets stronger, faster, and higher. You smile, and soon enough you can't hold it any longer and burst out with happy laughter. "Wheeeee!!!"

When swinging forward, you experience a powerful feeling of rising up and going high and higher. Swinging forward is all about joy, excitement, boldness, and wanting faster, higher, and more.

When swinging backwards, you experience a gain of enormous strength and power that you will use in your next swing forward to go even faster and higher. Swinging backwards is all about collecting and gaining might, and getting ready for the next powerful forward swing.

Both, swinging backward and forward, are a harmonious dance and both need the other to succeed.

In your new day, swing forward with joy and lots of "wheee's!" Have a blast, be excited and bold, and swing high and higher. But don't forget to let yourself swing back at times, to collect all your might, and gain infinite power for your next high forward swing.

That IS happiness!

Day 238

Put your hand over your heart and focus on your heart. Breathe and feel!

Say or think, "I am unconditional love!" Imagine your heart opening wide and its energy spreading into every cell of your body, mind, soul, and consciousness. If you like, play with that energy, swish it from side to side, and let it dance inside of you.

Then, visualize this energy spreading beyond your body, wider and further. Let it travel all around the world and then back to you. Feel your powerful shift to BE and live in the frequency of your heart.

Your heart is the most powerful energy-producing organ, and it gives birth to the mother of all good feelings; LOVE. When there is love, nothing less can exist which makes loving everything and everyone - including yourself - the most powerful answer there is.

Practicing unconditional self-love means you spread love to everyone and everything around you, and it makes it possible for you to love others unconditionally too.

That IS happiness!

Imagine a huge, amazing, majestic tree completely occupied by hundreds of black birds.

The tree seems happy and proud to host the huge community of birds. And the birds seem to be having a great time on that tree - and with each other - happily chirping loud and proud to one another. It is a picture of harmony, joy, and lots of fun.

Suddenly one bird flies off. All by itself. It flies up and down, left and right, and fast and slow. It seems to absolutely enjoy the playful time in the sky. It is amazing to watch!

There is a powerful message in this:

This bird is going for its truth by doing the only right thing there is: it takes off flying, all by itself, to make itself happy. It doesn't mind all the other hundred birds who stay, happily hanging out, and producing happy noise together.

Be that ONE bird for yourself in your new day!

That IS happiness!

Day 240

Start a powerful and respectful companionship with your anger!

Anger is not always wanted and many times it's judged as bad—which is not the case at all. It is part of each one of us, just like happiness, and it has its role for us.

Anger is energy like everything else, it's just real powerful and forceful; and since anger is a part of you, you are this powerful and forceful energy. Just think how fast and how powerfully you can clean your house when you are angry.

To start this powerful companionship, give your anger its deserved space. Imagine inviting it inside of you and showing it to its own perfect room. That room has a door which you or your anger can close or open at any time. If you take good care of yourself, your anger hangs out happily inside its room, door closed, and has no need to pop its head out. Your anger only takes initiative to open the door and come out if you overstep your boundaries. Then you get angry. If so, ask your anger what just happened. Listen to your anger, because it has all the information on how your boundaries got overstepped and where you did not take good care of yourself.

Give your anger the respect it deserves! It is your great personal reminder to take exceptional care of yourself, and it is your personal infinite force of energy, meant to be used for yourself only, and never to be taken out on others.

Enjoy this powerful companionship!

That IS happiness!

Day 241

Imagine it is bedtime and you are about to go to sleep. The last thing you do is walk through your house, checking every room and tidying up little things here and there because you like waking up to a tidy place that welcomes you with freshness.

That cleansing practice initiates a clean and fresh sleep and awakening by shifting you to BE and live in a frequency of clear and new.

Tidying up your energy before you go to sleep will shift you to BE and live in that same frequency, initiating a clean and fresh sleep and an awakening filled with joy.

So here goes the energetic nighttime cleansing:

Think of all the un-fitting things in your life. Acknowledge them without getting emotionally involved and certainly refrain from judgment. Accept, respect, appreciate, thank, and love them for the gift they are. This removes all accumulated resistance. Feel your shift to BE and live in peace with all there is for you. Then move on...

Think of all fitting in your life. Acknowledge it and indulge in feeling it fully. Bathe in it and fill every cell of your body, mind, soul, and consciousness with this goodness. Feel your shift to BE and live in your high-for-life frequency. Enjoy this and when ready move on...

Think of what and how you want your life to be. See, hear, smell, taste, think, and feel it without limits. Indulge in this high-for-life visualization and smile.

Last thought before you fall asleep is "I am grateful for everything!" Your heart is full! Your sleep is sweet!

That IS happiness!

Day 242

You can ALWAYS be with yourself!

Make it a regular practice to spend time with yourself without any distractions. Sit alone in quiet with nothing to do, nothing to listen to, and nothing to look at. Just you, right here and now, being with yourself.

Then have an honest conversation:

Ask yourself "How does my body feel? How does my heart feel? How is my mind doing? What are my feelings? What is going on in me?"

Feel and acknowledge everything coming up for you without judgment. There is no right or wrong, and no good or bad. It all just IS. Accept, respect, appreciate, thank, and love it all as it IS.

Practicing this will gift you with knowledge, understanding, and wisdom. You will get to know yourself better and better and never ever feel lonely again. And the best part? You are in charge of how great of a time you want to have.

In your new day, make time to be with yourself and enjoy all these good times!

That IS happiness!

Day 243

Imagine your heart as a boundless, powerful, love-rocket producing engine. Wow!

These love rockets are stuffed with all your high-for-life feelings of love, light, and happiness. They are always ready to launch. Visualize one of your love rockets and feel the healing power it contains.

Now imagine launching these rockets, one by one:

- Into places in your physical body in need of healing. Visualize them arriving at their destination and healing right there on the spot. Feel this!
- Into your mind, to meet your negative thoughts. Visualize the rockets infusing all negativity with love, happiness, and good feeling thoughts. Feel this!
- Into your soul. Reminding you of the pure and infinite love and light you are. Feel this!
- Into consciousness, flooding everything in your NOW with magic. Feel this!

But wait, don't stop there!

Launch your love generously to everyone and everything, knowing that your heart simply produces more of these powerful love rockets for you to use.

That IS happiness!

Day 244

Being lighthearted, thinking light-mindedly, and feeling light-weighted shifts you to BE and live in a frequency of lightness. So light, you can almost fly.

Here is what shifts you to BE and live in your lightness:

- Saying or thinking "I am lightness! You are lightness! All is lightness!"
- Laughing, playing, and goofing off.
- Putting on clothing and shoes that feel light, eat light food, and do physical activities that make you feel light.
- Noticing all lightness around you: in feathers, light fabrics, fluffs, cotton balls, and cotton candy.

Go find all the dust bunnies in your home; they are your best *lightness-shifters*. Play with them, blow on them, watch them be light, and enjoy your shift and creation of laughter.

That IS happiness!

Day 245

Imagine you get yourself something nice to drink.

Whether it's hot tea or a glass of wine, choose what fits. You pair it with some delicious food. You prepare your comfy sofa with fluffy pillows and a soft blanket. You light a candle and snuggle up. You are beyond excited to observe this breathtaking movie that is about to play for you.

You hit play. The opening picture is a stunning scenery accompanied by beautiful music. And then the title appears:

The Story of Your Phenomenal Life!

Wow! Please sit back and enjoy being the observer of:

- All you have made possible, were open to receive, have accomplished and experienced, have overcome, created, and enjoyed in your phenomenal life.
- All you have seen, heard, felt, thought, smelled, and tasted in your magnificent life.
- All you have been so far, and ARE now.

Watch this best-ever movie with admiration for the main character, YOU!

Celebrate yourself infinitely! You have done amazing and are remarkable. Just watch your movie!

That IS happiness!

Day 246

Coating everything that is happening with playfulness, well, makes it all playful!

When something un-fitting happens, acknowledge your immediate reaction, no matter what it is. Accept, respect, appreciate, thank, and love your first feeling. Then imagine coating the happening with playfulness, just as chocolate syrup coats ice-cream. That shifts you to BE and live in a playful frequency, where you can be open and receiving for fitting solutions.

Who knows, by the time your shift to playfulness is complete, the happening might not even be a happening anymore - life is an ever-changing and ever-moving experience - but you still win, because at the end you are in a playful mood.

Being playful exercises your trust: trust in yourself that you are capable and deserving, trust that what's happening is right for you, trust that you are taken care off, and trust that you can smile and laugh about anything.

Playfulness is worth coating your life with!

That IS happiness!

Day 247

Imagine that you are on a mission to make space for your truth!

First, be open and love all that is there for you, especially who or what may be un fitting. Think or say "I love you!" to the ground, the walls, the air, all people, and all happenings. Let go of all resistance and grow the biggest power you possess: your love. Think of it as acknowledging the un-fitting and dipping it into your powerful love.

Next, imagine blessing everyone standing in the way of experiencing a spectacular time. Without getting emotionally entangled or judging, move them gently out of your way. Remember, this only happens in your imagination. Nobody gets hurt and nobody will ever know. This is an inside cleaning job, not an issue-solving exercise.

Finally, welcome yourself into your all-loving and resistance-free space by enjoying a straight view of a spectacular life. It is time to BE and live your truth: to believe in yourself, and to celebrate all that you are. Then proudly march forward to your own magnificent rhythm that is so abundant and joyous for you.

That IS happiness!

Day 248

I see the best in me. I see the best in you. You see the best in you. You see the best in me. On and on this goes!

Look into your magic mirror and see all of your beauty and uniqueness. Admire and think fondly of yourself; how smart, genuine, and inspiring you are. Then recall all the amazing things you have already lived and experienced. Consciously see, feel, hear, speak, and think about all that "best" in and about you.

Then, turn towards everyone and everything. Look at them—and see their beauty and uniqueness. Admire and think fondly of them; how smart, genuine and inspiring they are. Recall all the amazing things they have already lived and experienced. Consciously see, feel, hear, speak, and think about all that is "best" in them, and about them.

This brings the focus onto the "best" in yourself, everyone, and everything, which shifts all to BE and live in a high-for-life frequency.

That IS happiness!

Day 249

Imagine you have a planting tray. Each compartment has a different kind of seed planted inside, every seed has its own space to grow, and none get mixed up; and yet, they are all connected, because of the tray. Every day you check on all the seeds, water them, make sure they get sunlight, and are warm. You have absolute trust and belief in them that they have their own power and wisdom to grow. If they do well, you watch their growth with joy. If they don't do well, you adjust the water-giving, warmth and sun-intake. Never would you lose your trust in them, or get all tangled up in their business of growing. Rather, you keep faith in their own reason to BE.

The same goes for your loved ones. Think of every loved one as a seed living in a compartment of a planting tray. Every person gets their own space to grow without getting mixed up, yet everyone is connected. You check on everyone daily, nurture them with compassion, love, your light, well wishes, and your happiness. You have absolute trust and belief in every single one that they have their own power and wisdom to grow, be well, and live happy. If they do well, you watch their growth with excitement. If they don't do well, you adjust your way of nurturing. Never will you lose your trust in them or get all tangled up in their business of living. You keep faith in their own reason to BE. The best thing you can do for yourself, everyone, and all is to not get tangled up in anyone's life-business. Instead gift them with your unconditional trust and belief in them, then turn towards yourself and take care of your own life-business. Which is to be the happiest, healthiest, loving, and purest YOU, that you can be.

That IS happiness!

Day 250

Happy mindfulness!

Being mindful means you consciously acknowledge all that is there for you *right now*. In good times it is easy, because you love focusing on all the happiness that is there. It is the hard times when being mindful becomes hard to practice.

In those days, acknowledge everything without judgment. Then accept, respect, appreciate, thank, and love it all. Next, ask yourself: "What happiness can I mindfully feel right now, to shift myself to BE and live mindfully happy?"

For example:

If you have physical pain, acknowledge it. Accept, respect, appreciate, thank, and love your pain for the communication it brings. Then find something in your body that represents happiness, and mindfully focus on that. Take, for instance your smile. Mindfully focus on your smile! This will create happy energy in you which you will fill every cell of your body with, initiating health and healing.

Practice happy mindfulness at all times!

That IS happiness!

Day 251

When a loved one has a hard time, you show them compassion and care.

You connect with their heart by offering your help, time, and a listening ear. You remind them how wonderful they are. You shower and envelope them in your love and light. You tell them they are not alone and that everything is OK. You advise them to be gentle, understanding, and forgiving towards themselves. Not to care what others think or say, but stay true to themselves. And most likely, you pamper and spoil them with goodies and *yummies*.

That makes your loved one feel good - it makes you feel good - and it shifts the situation to goodness.

Now imagine that you are the one having a hard time.

What is your reaction towards yourself? Are you hard, unforgiving? Do you talk or think negatively about yourself?

If so, it's about high time to replace your old, unloving, and worn-out reactions towards yourself with new and nourishing "feel good" thoughts FOR yourself.

Treat yourself as you would treat your loved one. Accept, respect, appreciate, thank, love, and honor yourself in the same way—feel compassion, and shower yourself with your love!

The whole world wins that way!

That IS happiness!

Day 252

Love is everywhere, so tune into it!

Consciously see, hear, taste, smell, think, and feel all the love that is present in and around you:

- FEEL your heart being wide open, producing, spreading, and receiving love.
- SEE love in everything and everyone you encounter, including yourself.
- SMELL love in every delicious scent.
- HEAR love in every noise and sound.
- TASTE love in all the *yumminess* that you indulge in.
- THINK "I love you!" towards everything and everyone, including yourself.

Notice all heart shapes popping up for you: they carry the energy of love and are love reminders for you to BE and live in the frequency of your grandest energy and power—your love!

Let your love - and the love of others - make your heart skip and jump today!

That IS happiness!

Day 253

Imagine that you are looking at all of the clouds in the sky.

Pick the one you love the most, then fly yourself right up to it. You are now floating in front of your beautiful cloud. You see there is a door. You open it, and slip into a huge empty space inside of your cloud. You close the door. You are all alone. There is no noise, no view, no smell, no taste, no thoughts, and no feelings present. It is completely "sound-view-smell-taste-thought-and-feeling-proof" in there. You sit down and breathe.

Welcome to your nothing space!

That nothing space is where you can ask any questions you may have about anything. It is where you can hear all your answers loud and clear. That nothing space is where your own clarity lives.

Looking for answers outside of your nothing space will never get you pure information because all of the answers from outside come loaded with other people's energies; feelings, opinions, judgments, *wantings*, and old beliefs. Making them impure.

Looking for answers within will always get you the purest guidance for yourself. Then you can act, and make fitting changes for you.

So go, be in your cloud often!

That IS happiness!

Day 254

Picture a smiley face that makes you feel happy and joyous!

Feel this for a little. If you like, draw it onto a post-it and keep it with you in your new day as a happiness reminder and a smile inducer.

Now copy your smiley face onto and into everything and everyone:

- See that smiley face in and on water before you drink it.
- Picture it in and on your food before your eat.
- Imagine it on walls in your house and at work.
- In your mind draw it onto people's faces.
- Make an imaginary sketch of that smiley face on the ground beneath every step that you take.

Every time you imagine that smiley face it shifts you - as well as what and whom you project it on - to BE and live in that happy, joyous frequency you felt when you pictured it. You re-live your earlier feelings.

This results in a constant happiness creation in and for you. Plus, think about all of the playfulness and smiles you call into life.

That IS happiness!

Day 255

Imagine that you are planning a magnificent gathering to cele-brate life.

You choose the location, decoration, food, and drinks. You send out beautiful invitations. All is ready and set to go. You are so excited!

However, on that special day, the weather is not cooperating at all. You decide to move the date so that the celebration can be amazing value and fun. All is good.

The new day arrives with weather even more severe this time. With a sigh, you consider moving it again, but decide against it. You realize, instead of basing the value and fun of this celebration on the weather, you want to base it on you - and how you see, hear, taste, smell, think, and feel about it. You come to understand that good and bad weather is actually part of that exact life you want to celebrate. It has no impact on the success, because you choose to have a blast no matter what; and that is what your gathering was, a blast!

Your new day is that gathering to celebrate your life!

You can experience it in two ways:

You can base the quality and fun on the weather, other people, and happenings outside of your control. You could keep moving your celebration of life further out, day by day, until the conditions are perfect. "I will be happy tomorrow, when things are better."

Or...

You can decide that you're in charge to make your new day happen. Instead of basing the quality and fun on other people and happenings, you base it on you, and how you see, hear, taste, smell, think, and feel about living your new day. Fitting and non fitting are both important parts of that exact day you are gifted to experience and celebrate.

I count on you to choose the latter!

You deserve to have a blast at your magnificent gathering!

That IS happiness!

Day 256

"I love!"

Those words carry the energy of love, compassion, joy, abundance, and happiness. Saying and thinking "I love!" shifts you to BE and live in that high-for-life frequency. For example:

"I love doing chores" shifts you and your chores to BE and live in a frequency of love. Making chores lovable and fun. Hey, you might even smile.

"I love snuggling my pets" shifts you and your pets to BE and live in a state of love. Decorating the love already created, simply by snuggling with your pets. Very powerful goodness!

"I love driving this car" shifts you and your car to BE and live in an energy of love. A safe frequency, because there is no negativity, agitation, or resistance present. You drive safe and your car is safe. Remember, you and your car are both energy, connected, and share your energies with each other.

"I love everything" shifts you and everything to BE and live in a frequency of love. Magical!

Be an "I love!" spreader in your new day!

That IS happiness!

Day 257

Imagine that you are at an outdoor market to buy fresh produce.

You pause to take in the beautiful sight of this delicious food. You are very excited, because you get to go and choose the produce that looks the best to you and will make you the happiest.

You walk to the first stand, pause, and look at all produce that this stand is offering. Some of it looks and feels super fresh, and some does not. You pick the freshest, pay, and move to the next stand. You shop like this until the last stand. When finished, you look at your bag which is filled with the freshest and most feel-good produce you could find. You smile and feel so good.

The reason you feel so good is because you chose what looked and felt good to you and respectfully declined what did not look and feel good to you.

Life invites you to do exactly that, and here is how:

Acknowledge everything in your awareness, just like you acknowledged all of the produce at that market. Without looking at everything, you can't choose what makes you feel good. Accept, respect, appreciate, thank, and love all the variety.

Time to pick and choose! Fill your "bag of life" with all that feels good for you. Take it home and indulge in it. Respectfully decline all that is not feeling good for you. Leave it behind and out of your "bag of life."

Once in a while look at your full "bag of life" Be grateful and smile! Have pride in yourself that you are a picky chooser about what goes into your "bag of life"!

That IS happiness!

Day 258

Seriously, don't take everything so seriously!

The word "serious" caries an energy of meaning business, sternness, danger and don't play/smile/laugh/joke. Being serious and using the word serious shifts you to BE and live in that frequency.

Versus...

Not serious. Lighthearted. That carries the energy of lightness, fun, playfulness, laughter, jokes, being free, and goofing off. Being, saying, or thinking "lighthearted" shifts you to BE and live in that fun frequency.

So be aware of your thoughts, feelings, and reactions towards yourself, everyone, and everything. Are they too serious? If so, shift to play and laughter and watch how you, everything, and everyone become lighter.

Also notice all lightheartedness and *un-seriousness* around you. Watch children play and happy people laugh, and feel your shift to BE and live in that same light state.

Seriously, consider it!

That IS happiness!

Day 259

Imagine a piece of metal in the sun, it is all bright and shiny!

"Shiny" carries the energy of special, luxurious, glamorous, grand, regal, beautiful, bright, and powerful. Saying or thinking the word "shiny" to yourself or others shifts you to BE and live in a bright frequency.

Indulging in, noticing, and focusing on all *shiny-ness*, be it people or things, gets you into that goodness too. Like:

- Dressing in shiny clothes and shoes.
- Eating and drinking shiny food.
- Watching shiny movies.
- Looking at shiny pictures, candles, and lamps.

Move yourself to BE and live in the frequency of your shiny you, and be a super shiner!

That IS happiness!

Day 260

Take 3!

Think of when you listen to a song you like, watch a small child, see a furry animal, or receive a compliment or fantastic news. Your heart is touched and opens up wide in these moments. You feel so much love and see so much goodness.

Pause for 3 minutes at a time in your new day. Pull yourself into your heart space with your thoughts, feelings, and energy. If it helps, touch your heart with your hands. Then, focus on something that moves and touches your heart. This can be a deep breath, a beautiful song, a decadent smell or taste, an imagination you love, a picture on your phone, or any memory that shifts you into your heart. Feel it for 3 minutes. Breathe! And off you go, hustling and bustling in your new day again.

This shifts you to BE and live in your heart space, fills your heart with love, and lets you see, feel, hear, taste, smell, and think of yourself, everything, and everyone through your heart-love lenses.

Take your 3 often.

That IS happiness!

Day 261

Imagine you are planning a fun party, but only you show up.

Now don't get me wrong, you showing up means the most important person is present, because it's your party and your intend to have a fun time. So naturally you will, even it's only you.

But wouldn't it be more interesting to have more people coming? Maybe even some add-ons you don't know. Wouldn't that spice up your party with surprise and adventure?

Think of your new day as your fun party you are about to experience.

Spending it alone sometimes is needed and gives you a magnificent time. But more often than not, it is amazing to spend your new day in company of others; some loved and others not so loved. The loved ones help create a fun party. And the not so loved ones create contrast for you which brings clarity and is magic in itself.

Your life becomes vivid and colorful if you spend your party out and about with others, because together you co-create what you cannot create on your own.

Sometimes it takes more than one!

That IS happiness!

Day 262

Think of water and how it moves around rocks.

It always finds a way to flow around, above, and even underneath them. Water flows wherever it wants to flow, and does not stop or get held up by the rocks. It keeps its focus on its purpose to flow, and finds other ways around blockages to stay true to itself.

You ARE that same flow! You are mostly made of water, which means you are mostly flow.

To stay true to your flow, don't make the rocks in your life the most important happenings. Instead, keep your focus on your purpose to flow, and with that, find other ways around them to be and live your truth.

Being in your flow means to BE and live in a frequency of feeling good and resistance free. You don't fight, but welcome everything that is happening for you. You accept, respect, appreciate, thank, and love everything that is for you.

For example: Let's say you get angry. Acknowledge your anger. Accept, respect, appreciate, thank, and love it. Tell your anger it can stay as long as it needs to stay. You, on the anther hand, will move on in your new day, knowing that it is present, but refrain from joining it to have a tea party and talk in detail about the "why." That lets your anger be as is, without making it the most important rock of your moment. You simply flow around it and shift back to BE and live in your high-for-life frequency of flow and happiness.

That IS happiness!

Day 263

Imagine that you get to go on a trip to the destination of your choice!

Now comes the big question; Where to?

To find the where, you ask yourself how you want to feel on that trip. What kind of environment feels good. What kind of happiness you are looking for. What kind of food you desire. What kind of smells you like. What kind of sounds you want to listen to, and what your expectations are to have the best trip ever.

You visualize yourself in different places and feel, see, hear, taste, smell, and think of yourself being there. With the resulting clarity you start planning your perfect trip.

Put that same planning effort into your new day, because your new day is like that trip. You get to choose where and how it will be.

Ask yourself :

- How do you want to feel in this new day?
- What kind of environment feels good?
- What kind of happiness are you looking for?
- What kind of food do you desire?
- What kind of smells and sounds do you want?
- What are your expectations to feel amazing and have the best day ever?

With the resulting clarity, go into your new day and enjoy your trip!

That IS happiness!

Day 264

Everything just IS!

The good, the bad, the sad, the joyous, the harsh, the angry, and the happy are all the same until you decide how you feel about it. Think about it—what feels good to you might feel bad to others, and what feels bad to you now might feel like a blessing later.

So why not at first acknowledge everything simply as IS?

Then accept, respect, appreciate, thank, and love all that IS for you as a gift, because everything in your awareness is meant for you to experience. Everything is available for you to get closer to yourself, gain understanding and wisdom, and find clarity in what you want and what you don't want, which makes everything that IS, a gift for you.

Enjoy!

And imagine all the fun you will have when opening all these personalized gifts. It will feel like it's your birthday!

That IS happiness!

Day 265

Imagine a beautiful bird sitting on a branch of a giant tree.

After a while, the bird opens its wings to fly to a lower branch of a neighbor tree. It takes off effortlessly, flies free as can be, and lands smoothly on the new branch.

That bird took off with complete trust in its flying skills—the natural thing for it to do. It trusted that it would land on that new branch and that it would be strong and good enough to carry it, and if there is trouble, there will be another branch.

It had its intentions set, knew how to use the natural skills, and trusted in the process by knowing it will be fine and taken care of.

The natural thing for you to do is to live your life!

You can trust in your living skills, because living this life is your natural skill. You can trust you will always land on the branches you are supposed to land on, and that they are strong and capable enough to carry you; and in case of trouble, there is always another branch available and ready.

Set your intentions. Know that living is your natural skill. Trust in the process. Believe you will be fine and taken care of.

Life loves you, and the universe has your back!

That IS happiness!

Day 266

It is all about recycling!

Everything always starts in you: you have a wish in your heart, you think of it, you visualize it, you feel it, and the universe receives your wish. And voila, your wish manifests in your physical life. That is a simple and speedy explanation of how it works when you create from your heart and for your highest good.

Important is how you experience it once it's manifested!

If you look at your wish manifestation quickly and say "Oh, that is cool!" and move on without investing your feelings in it, it will be an *un-recycled* event. You will only get part of the experience.

But if you look at your wish manifestation and indulge with feeling, seeing, hearing, tasting, smelling, and thinking about how amazing this is for you, you recycle the energy of the manifestation you created. It fills every cell of your body, mind, soul, and consciousness, shifts you to BE and live in the high-for-life frequency, and sets the tone for your next. How you feel in your now creates the scenery for your next, and that is when you get the whole experience.

Be a committed *recycler*!

That IS happiness!

Day 267

Stop. Sit down. Breathe! Breathing deserves your undivided attention! It contains loads of information about how you are, and can be programmed with any high-for-life energy you wish to fill yourself with and shift to.

- You can *breathe* yourself into health and abundance.
- You can *breathe* yourself into peace and love.
- You can *breathe* yourself into anything you desire!

First, feel yourself breathing in and out: Do you feel tingling, peaceful, or energized? Does conscious breathing bring you a smile or tears? Do you feel your energy as still, spreading, or moving? Do you feel your heart opening wide and big when you breath in or out? Feel how you are! Next, program your breath by imagining:

- Breathing in love and breathing out anything not love.
- Breathing in health and breathing out all *un-healthy*.
- Breathing in vivid energy and breathing out all *non-vivid-ness*.
- Breathing in peace and breathing out all thoughts of non-peace.
- Breathing in abundance and breathing out all beliefs of non-abundance.

Breathing is life! You are life! You ARE your breath!

That IS happiness!

Day 268

Surrender!

Every night, you either get split-naked or put on your pajamas to go to bed. You go to the bed, the bed does not come to you. Then you hop in, lay down, close your eyes, and go to sleep. You surrender for (hopefully) many hours to your bed. You trust your bed fully and completely. You relax and recharge.

Think of this bed as your life!

It wants you to show up, hop in, completely surrender, and fully trust in all that it has to offer you. It wants you to relax and recharge so you can experience everything happening for you without fear, stress, or any other not-good-feeling energies.

What are you waiting for? Surrender!

You are an accomplished and trained *surrenderer*. Use that training!

That IS happiness!

Day 269

Stop searching for who you are!

First of all, since you are an ever-changing being living in an ever-changing universe, as soon as you find yourself it is old cake because within a second, that is not who you are anymore.

Second, what would you do anyways if you suddenly found yourself? Stop living, evolving, trying?

Third, what are you going do until you find yourself?

I believe that you are who you are right now, and that there is nothing to search for because you already found who you are. Just look at yourself, and feel, see, hear, taste, smell, and think of yourself right now. That is who you are!

- If you are angry right now, that is who you are.
- If you are sad right now, that is who you are.
- If you are stuck right now, that is who you are.
- If you are happy right now that is who you are.

Acknowledge, accept, respect, appreciate, thank and love who you are.

From there, keep following your heart's desire. Then realize that this is now who you are. Keep living!

I hope you give up the search to find yourself and instead just love yourself as who you are right now.

That IS happiness!

Day 270

Imagine that you just finished building your house.

You set the last piece of stone, painted the last stroke of color, and cleaned up the last piece of material around the house. You call everyone you know to come over and admire your finished house. Wow!

What a feeling of accomplishment, power, capability, and strength you are shifting to with this happening. A true high-for-life frequency to be and live in.

Good news...

You can feel good like that many times in your new day, because there are thousands of happenings you accomplish throughout your day. They just have become normal for you, so you don't consciously feel, see, hear, smell, taste, and think of them as accomplishments. I say don't rob yourself of feeling amazing a thousand times a day! They are ALL accomplishments, and you did accomplish them. So, bravo!

Notice when you make coffee, brush your teeth, make someone laugh, serve dinner, or clean the house. No matter how small, it is worth feeling amazing about your accomplishments.

If by any chance you have trouble feeling amazing about a super small accomplishment, simply go back to the imagination of "you just finished building your house." That will shift you to BE and live in your frequency of feeling amazing.

You are an accomplished being, and you deserve to feel that way!

That IS happiness!

Day 271

Think of - and feel - your feet!

Not only are your feet your grounding partners (because they ground you with every step that you take), they are also your deep feel-good partners, because every tickle, barefoot activity, skip, jump, rub and massage, foot bath, and creaming session shifts you to feeling good, being energized, and happy.

Grounding carries the energy of being connected; of knowing, wisdom, strength, security, trust, nourishment, balance, and pride for who you are. Feeling good carries the energy of health, happiness, abundance, love, peace, and relaxation. You get the idea of why your feet really deserve your pampering attention!

Send them your love, and thank them for doing the heavy carrying of walking your body everywhere. Then, lighten their load and nourish them with the following:

Feel the bottom of your feet. Acknowledge all non-fitting energies in you. Starting at your crown, let all these non-fitting energies flow downward through your body, out through the bottom of your feet. Clean out and let it all go!

Imagine Mother Earth offering you abundant amounts of nourishment. Gratefully accept and let all of this goodness flow in through the bottom of your feet, up your legs and into your crown.

Feel your feet smiling; their load got lighter because you are lighter, and their strength got bigger because they got nourishment.

That IS happiness!

Day 272

Love yourself enough to not lose yourself in caring for everything and everyone at all times!

Caring too much for others is exhausting and shifts you to a "not good feeling" frequency of helplessness, never enough, or resentment. It creates drama; which always gets you completely away from feeling good and living your truth. Plus, most of the time it's not your business to care that much and not in your control to fix it for them.

Instead show compassion, understanding, and shower them with your love. Trust in everyone and everything that they are OK because just like you, everyone has their inner guidance leading them to do what is best for them; just like you, they are in charge to change and heal themselves; and just like you, everyone is here to experience what is happening for them.

Love yourself enough, and share THAT goodness with them.
Love others enough by giving them the space to BE.

That IS happiness!

Day 273

Co-create magic with the weather! Notice the weather—see, hear, smell, taste, think, and feel its energy. Shift to BE and live in its offered high-for-life frequency. For example:

Rain carries the energy of cleansing, refreshing, and calming. Shift yourself to BE and live in that fresh frequency.

Thunder carries the energy of light, *electric-ness*, power, strength, and "I am the boss!" Shift to BE and live in that powerful frequency.

Snow carries the energy of purity, cleanliness, neutrality, quietness, and winter wonderland. Shift yourself to BE and live in that white and peaceful frequency.

Fog carries the energy of solitude, *alone-ness*, and nothing-ness. If you are surrounded by fog all you can see is right here. This initiates trust in the unknown and unseen. Shift to BE and live in that trusting frequency.

The ever-so-energizing sun carries the energy of warm, happy, and bright. It is gentle yet strong; don't underestimate its power if you misuse it. Shift yourself to BE and live in that bright frequency.

Clouds carry the energy of gray. They spark your creativity with letting you take initiative to color the sky as you like. Shift to BE and live in that super creative frequency.

Hail carries the energy of being playful. They playfully bounce off the ground, but not to be made fun of—these pellets of frozen rain can be feisty. Shift to BE and live in that frequency of balance.

That IS happiness!

Day 274

Imagine you are on a safari expedition. See, hear, taste, smell, feel, and think of that nature with all the magnificent wild animals. Breathtaking!

Your jeep comes to a halt. You look to your left and see a lion; then, you look to your right and see a gazelle. You consciously acknowledge both of these animals with their very different energies, and are in awe of their majestic and amazing beauty.

Both animals are inviting you to walk up close to them. To sit down. And to spend time with them. Which one will you join? You start thinking and feeling what it would mean for you to join the lion or the gazelle. You ask yourself:

- Which one feels safer to me?
- Which one is more fitting for me?
- Which one will make me feel better?

In this scenario you go into detail about how you feel, think, hear, taste, smell, and see this situation, so you can make the right choice for you and be sure about it.

You have that option and power for ANY scenario in your life! Your inner guidance, knowing, and wisdom are always available to go into detail about anything that is happening for you. You can always ask yourself questions about what is good for you. You can always make the right and fitting choice for you... and be sure about it.

Make it a priority to go into detail to make the fitting choices for you! So who will you join, the lion or the gazelle?

That IS happiness!

Day 275

Your lips are very powerful!

They can shift your feelings immediately with the shape they are in and since feelings are energy, your lips can shift your energy. You have some powerful lips there! Try this, close your eyes and focus on your lips, then:

- Have your lips go straight across your face. Feel your energy!
- Have your lips smile, corners pulled up. Feel this!
- Have your lips open in a big toothy smile, corners pulled up high! Feel this!
- Have your lips frown, corners pulled down. Feel this!
- Have your lips frown even more, corners pulled way down. Feel this!

These lip positions all feel very different, and shift you to BE and live in very different frequencies as well.

So keep pulling your lips upward into a smile often in your new day because when you smile you automatically shift to BE and live in your frequency of happiness.

Plus, your smile shares happiness with others and maybe even changes their day; and when you get a smile back, it's a gift straight to your heart.

That IS happiness!

Day 276

Imagine a clean, clear, and fresh stream.

See, hear, taste, smell, think, and feel how pure, healthy, and refreshing that water is.

Have a seat by that stream. Watch its clear water flow. Listen to the healing sounds that the water creates. Stick your finger into it and taste its freshness. Stick your nose over it and smell its pureness. Consciously think about, and feel that clean, clear, fresh, pure, healthy, and flowing stream.

Now imagine this stream is your clean, clear, and fresh energy stream inside of you. See, hear, taste, smell, think, and feel how pure, healthy, refreshing, and flowing your energy is.

Sit by your energy stream. Watch your clear energy flow. Listen to the healing sounds that your energy stream creates. Stick your finger into it and taste its freshness. Stick your nose over it and smell its pureness. Consciously think about, and feel your clean, clear, fresh, pure, healthy, and flowing energy stream.

This shifts you to BE and live in your clean, clear, and fresh frequency.

Imagine and feel this often in your new day to remind yourself of the potent and powerful energy stream inside of you.

Keep it clean and fresh!

That IS happiness!

Day 277

Words are energy!

Read the following and hear yourself saying these words—feel the difference:

This is coffee.
This is *heavenly* coffee.

This is a bed.
This is an *energizing* bed.

This is a car.
This is a *fabulous* car.

This is water.
This is *pure* and *healing* water.

Using uplifting words shift you and whatever or whomever you talk about, to BE and live in a high-for-life frequency. And as this uplifting team, you will share this goodness; spreading it wider and wider. Everything is energy, connected, and shares its energies.

Uplifting words change energy, which means they change everything!

That IS happiness!

Day 278

Imagine a breathtakingly beautiful flower tells you all about the parts it does not like on itself, or finds ugly.

What would you say to that flower?

You would look at it and tell it that what you see is breathtakingly beautiful. That all parts belong together and create its beauty. You would do anything in your power to show it understanding, compassion, and love, to try to shift it to accept, respect, appreciate, thank, and love every part because all parts deserve to be loved, no?

Now imagine a breathtakingly beautiful YOU. Talking about all parts you don't like on yourself, or find ugly. What would you say to yourself?

You deserve the same words you gave that flower, because everything you said is your truth too. You are breathtakingly beautiful! All of your parts belong together, creating your beauty. You deserve to give yourself all the understanding, compassion, and love—and shift yourself to accept, respect, appreciate, thank and love every part of you because all parts of you deserve to be cherished.

That IS happiness!

Day 279

Feel yourself in love!

Visualize how over the moon happy you are, how amazingly healthy you feel, how fantastically energized you are, and how much you want to hug the whole world. Life is a joy.

Now imagine the person that you are so smitten with is you. You read right! YOU are in love with YOU!

Self-love is the most important love there is. It shifts you to BE and live in your frequency of your heart, your light, your health, your happiness and your truth.

Self-love is:

- YOU acknowledging YOU!
- YOU accepting YOU!
- YOU respecting YOU!
- YOU appreciating YOU!
- YOU thanking YOU!
- YOU loving YOU!

It means you commit to make "feeling good" your number one priority through:

- Taking exceptional care of your body by choosing clean food, exercising, drinking plenty of water, and getting good sleep.
- Taking exceptional care of your mind by thinking clean and good feeling thoughts.
- Taking exceptional care of your soul by keeping your energy clean and pure and staying connected with who you are.

- Keeping your focus on what is going right for you right now and practice feeling gratitude for that.

Self-love is to celebrate your power, beauty, and the abundance that you are, and honor yourself with your love for YOU!

That IS happiness!

Day 280

Imagine that you are in a row boat on a river.

First you go with its flow. Down the river. It is easy to steer and row your boat. Then it is time to go back. You row your boat up the river, against its flow. It is really hard and exhausting to steer and row that way.

That is the same in your new day!

It will be a pleasant and resistance-free experience if you get yourself into the flow, and steer and row in the same direction with what is happening for you; versus rowing and steering against what is happening for you and the flow it offers.

Rowing and flowing with your new day means that you acknowledge, accept, respect, appreciate, thank, and love all that is happening for you. From that state, you will be able to create your desired change and receive all the goodness that is ready for you.

So row, row, row your boat gently DOWN THE STREAM...

With the flow!

That IS happiness!

Day 281

Don't be afraid to live fully because you are afraid to die!

You are a soul having a physical experience. That physical experience is going to change at some point. It is a transition between dimensions and a beginning of new.

Fear of dying means you are fearing your transition and the beginning of your new. It holds you back from experiencing your life fully, because it creates your fear of living vividly. "What if something happens?"

With practicing trust in your transition and your new beginning, the fear of dying disappears... And without the fear to die, the fear of living vividly, cannot exist.

Without those two kinds of fears, you will go and take part in adventures, eat that super spicy food, drive that race car, go on that bike ride in the mountains, and try that skateboard jump you always wanted to.

You will shift to BE and live in your high-for-life frequency and will reveal to everyone and everything around you that life is meant to see, hear, taste, smell, think, and feel fully and vividly.

Happiness is to live without fear!

That IS happiness!

Day 282

Be flexible!

The weather's got you trained well. It keeps you flexible and open to the unknown. Sure, you can watch the forecast, but can you really count on it? No! To experience your days in a feel-good way you have to stay flexible and trust that you will be able to adjust to whatever weather conditions come your way.

Use that training in your new day to experience everything and everyone in a feel-good way!

Stay flexible and open to the unknown. Trust that you will be able to adjust to whatever life conditions come your way. And make peace with the understanding that even if some experiences might be in the forecast (and you can prepare for them), you can not always count on them.

That is life's way of training you well!

That IS happiness!

Day 283

A life full of wonders is a wonderful life!

The word "wonder" carries the energy of magic, miracles, limitless, curiosity, special, and out of this world. Noticing and consciously seeing, hearing, tasting, smelling, thinking, and feeling all wonder that is present shifts you to BE and live in a high-for-life frequency.

What if I told you that there are wonders present in you, everything, everyone, and everywhere, in every split second there is? It would mean that it's possible for you to BE and live in a frequency of wonder all the time. Yes?

Well...

You are wonder. Your love is wonder. Your family and children are wonder. Nature and animals are wonder. Cities are wonder. Every smile you give and receive is wonder. Every breath and step you take is wonder. Our universe is wonder. Even someone you are not fond of is wonder.

Pause often in your new day, consciously celebrate all wonder in you and around you.

Wonder-full!

That IS happiness!

Day 284

Imagine that you are sitting down on a comfy sofa. You relax and smile. Your eyes are wide open. You start looking around and acknowledge everything and everyone you see (no matter how you feel about them or it) with saying or thinking "Thank you!"

This lets you honor everything and everyone with gratitude. No matter the feeling you have towards them. This lets you see, hear, taste, smell, feel, and think beyond your perceptions. You let go of any resistance you have, and you shift to BE and live in a frequency of thankfulness. That is where health, abundance, love, and happiness can exist.

In your new day, imagine yourself sitting on your thankfulness sofa often:

- Acknowledge all beauty. Say "Thank you!"
- Acknowledge all non-fitting happenings and people. Say "Thank you!"
- Acknowledge all light. Say "Thank you!"
- Acknowledge all dark. Say "Thank you!"
- Acknowledge all happiness. Say "Thank you!"

Talk about a day-changer!

That IS happiness!

Day 285

A great script makes a great movie. A great movie is a great experience and a great experience is happiness.

Imagine that you are writing a script for your new day. Naturally, you choose to write a great script because that will make for a great day, a great experience, and enormous happiness.

So get scripting! Just remember, this is your great movie, so stick to positivity only.

Script how you want your new day to be; how happy you want to feel, and a high-for-life version of all non-fitting in your life. Once done, visualize and feel, see, hear, taste, smell, and think of what you scripted in a very vivid way. This shifts you to BE and live in your desired frequency of your script, setting a manifesting tone for your new day.

Re-live your script often in your new day, be the main star, and live in your high-for-life movie!

That IS happiness!

Day 286

Imagine that you live on a huge magnificent estate with a humongous mansion.

There are plenty of bedrooms, bathrooms, and many entertainment rooms; a dining hall, ballroom, cinema, spa, swimming pool, indoor sports facilities, bowling arena, pool table room, and a casino. And not to forget, the amazing chef's kitchen.

The outdoors are just as amazing. There are endless acres of breathtaking nature, including a beach, forest, and organic farmland. There is a golf course, a horse stable, outside sports facilities, and an outdoor pool.

Anything you can possibly think of is right there and always available to give you a fantastic experience and to make you feel happy. Would you ever leave that paradise to find happiness outside of that estate?

Your physical body, mind, soul, and consciousness are like that estate—a paradise!

Your physical body has everything you need to be happy. It is designed to give you a vivid, adventurous, moving, energized, and active life experience. It wants you to feel happy.

Your mind has everything you need to be happy. It entertains you with incredible thoughts and imaginations that want you to be happy.

Your soul has everything you need to be happy. It loves to connect with you, and be heard to teach you and help you grow. It wants you to be happy and experience a joyful life.

And consciousness has everything you need to be happy. It lets you experience your NOW—your personal happy place. Just think of experiencing your breath (which is your NOW) that can be felt as your personal happiness.

You have all that you will ever need to BE happy, inside of your paradisal estate.

That IS happiness!

Day 287

Pick a feel-good word that touches your heart.

It can be "love", "peace", "happiness," the list goes on. Close your eyes, say or think your chosen word, and feel your shift to BE and live in the frequency of that word.

Then, go on in your new day, seeing, thinking, hearing, tasting, smelling, and feeling that word in yourself, everything, and everyone you encounter.

For example:

If you chose "peace," see peace in yourself when you look in the mirror. Feel peace in people around you. Taste and smell peace in your food and drinks. Hear peace in sounds surrounding you and think peace in your mind.

Practice all peace initiating activities. Notice where the word "peace" itself is written. And focus on all peace in everything and everyone around you.

This shifts you to BE and live in a frequency of peace, which creates a peaceful stage for you and others to experience a peaceful day.

That IS happiness!

Day 288

Imagine that you are taking a shower or bubble bath, and a round bit of fluffy foam lands on your nose.

What do you do?

You immediately cross your eyes and look at it. You smile, laugh, and feel like you are wearing a clown nose. Which makes you smile and laugh even more.

Foam carries the energy of light, playfulness, happiness, fun, and *airy-ness*. Playing with - and imagining - foam shifts you to BE and live in that playful frequency. Crossing your eyes naturally shifts you to an energy of smiles, laughter, fun, and play. A clown nose carries the energy of, well, a clown!

This little imagination carries a ton of high-for-life energies that shift you to BE and live in a frequency of happiness. So your prescription for the day is to imagine this often!

Add a spontaneous foam fight, crossing your eyes contest, or clown act competition and you have the recipe for a guaranteed jolly day.

If you can, get a clown nose. It's a great happiness, smile, and laughing initiator tool to have on hand.

That IS happiness!

Day 289

Start a close, loving, and nurturing relationship with your sadness.

Imagine that everyone has a love tank. It is where you store your love; for yourself, your life, others and everything. Depending on usage and re-fills, that love tank changes its level (with high and overflowing being the most elevated state you can be in).

Your sadness is your true gas meter that your love tank is low or maybe even empty. Time to re-fill!

The first step is to respond to your sadness with your judgmental-free acknowledgment.

The next step is to accept your sadness as your love tank meter. Respect it as the great reminder it is, appreciate it for helping you stay on track, thank it for watching over you, and love it to the moon and back for being a beautiful part of you. Shift your relationship with your sadness from "being sad is wrong" to "being sad is a healthy part of me."

Then it's time for a chit-chat with your sadness. Ask what it is you need. Listen with your heart wide open, because your sadness always knows and answers. Is it a healing hug, yoga or meditation, a walk in nature, a comforting meal, a trip to the massage salon, a festive outing, or a vacation that you are in need of? Or would serving others fill your love tank?

Follow the guidance of your sadness. Re-fill your love tank and let it overflow, then bathe in it, and shower everything and everyone with your overflow.

You and your sadness! A true love story!

That IS happiness!

Day 290

Imagine that you are walking on the street, and an autumn leaf is blowing behind you.

Hear and feel the sound it makes!

Now you can either simply say "Oh, it is just a leaf." Or you can start imagining this leaf is playing tag with you. It is running behind to get you! Feel yourself shift into playfulness, and notice your smile growing big while picturing this.

"Playful" carries an energy of being worry-free, light, child-like, creative, abundance, health, and youth. Being in a playful energy means you are in a healthy and happy high-for-life frequency.

The best is that there are millions of play-creating opportunities wanting to play with you, which means that if you are open, you can experience play a million times a day.

What are you waiting for? Catch them and play!

That IS happiness!

Day 291

You and water!

If you strengthen your relationship with water you automatically strengthen your connection with your natural flow!

Your physical body is mostly made of water. So naturally you have a high propensity of being in the flow, because water is the energy of flow. Key is to be conscious about it.

Being and living in your flow means that you experience everything with ease. You can crack a smile in your hardest times, laugh out loud when it seems impossible, and love when you feel like nothing is left.

I invite you to live your flow as often as you can with:

Visualizing your water and feel it flushing and gushing through your body. Say or think "I love you!" to your water. This creates a loving environment in which flow can be lived easily. Feel this!

Drinking plenty of water that you bless with "I love you!" before it enters your body. Feel how this water fills every cell of yours with flow and the love you programmed it with.

Plus, hang out and play consciously with water; go swimming, wash dishes, or take a shower. Feel and watch the natural flow of water. It initiates you feeling your flow.

Be your flow!

That IS happiness!

Day 292

Imagine that you admire something in a person. Then you realize that what you're admiring, you have as well. You go ahead and admire it in you too. All this admiration shifts you and the person you admire, to BE and live in a high-for-life frequency.

Now imagine that you judge something you don't admire in a person. Judging them means you judge yourself too, because everyone and everything have all the same components in them. How you live with them is the only difference. All this judging shifts you and that person you are judging to BE and live in a frequency of judgment. A better way would be to bless something you don't admire in a person. With doing so you bless it in yourself too. That makes for a resistance-free living towards yourself and others, and shifts you and that person to BE and live in the frequency of your blessings.

Admiring components that resonate with you means you admire those components in yourself too. Blessing components that don't resonate with you means you bless those components in yourself as well. For example:

- Water is flow. Admire its flow—admire your flow.
- Honey is sweet. Admire that sweetness! With that, you admire that exact sweetness in you too.
- The bus driver that is angry. Bless his anger! With that you bless your anger too.
- Chocolate is deliciously decadent. Admire that! With that you admire your deliciously decadent happiness in you too.

That IS happiness!

Day 293

How much "play" can you find in your new day?

Play is everywhere! It carries the energy of being playful, light, happy, young, and fun; of laughter and joy. The more you can see, hear, smell, taste, feel, and think of play the more fun your life gets. Because you shift to BE and live in a high-for-life frequency of play.

Become aware of all your play:

- Feel your heart's playful rhythm.
- See your eyes playful sparkles.
- Hear your playful laughter and voice.
- Notice your playfulness when you dance and skip.

Also look for all play around you: in others, balls, toys, playing children, birds flying in the wind, playful music, colors, foods, drinks, and playful clothing. Look for the word "play' written everywhere. All of these shift you to a playful frequency.

Plus, find and hang out with everything and everyone that is play, and join their play!

Play is where all the fun is!

That IS happiness!

Day 294

Imagine a beautiful book holding all of your past happenings.

Every moment that just WAS is written on a new page - filling your book constantly, and leaving your NOW clean and clear for you to live without any *impure-ness* of your WAS. You get to experience every moment that IS as the brand-new gift it is meant to be.

If, for any reason you ever want to go back to your WAS, you simply open the book. Do what you came to do. Close the book when done, and leave everything that WAS behind in your book. Then, shift back to your NOW as a clean and clear being.

There is no need to carry anything OLD with you into your NOW, but many reasons to leave everything that WAS behind so that you can experience your NOW clean and clear.

Take that book offer, because your beautiful book is happy to take all your WAS, keep it safe for you, and welcome you back with a smile if you ever have the need to re-visit.

That IS happiness!

Day 295

Start a truthful and honest relationship with your jealousy!

Jealousy is personal and different for everyone. You cannot share your jealousy or make others jealous too, like you can share your anger or make others angry too.

Your jealousy is your truth and insight into what you want - and need - to do for yourself to fulfill your desires. It's simple: If you ever don't know what you want, find what you are jealous about. Because that is what you want and then take action.

The important thing is to refrain from judging yourself or others for being jealous. Instead acknowledge, accept, respect, appreciate, thank, and love it for the great "truth tool" it is. Thank the person, situation, or thing for mirroring you your desires.

This is jealousy, felt and celebrated as the goodness it is, shifting you to BE and live in a high-for-life frequency!

Happy *jealous-ing*!

That IS happiness!

Day 296

Imagine you are in an empty theater choosing the perfect seat.

Your goal is to get the best view possible of the play that is about to start.

- Do you move closer to get a good close-up look of what is going on?
- Do you move farther away to get a clear view of the whole picture?
- Or do you move to the side to get a different perspective?

You base your choice on your personal preferences and what feels good to you. And you count on being flexible enough to switch your seat if needed.

Live your new day as if it were that play. Choose where you want to be in order to experience everything at all times in the best way and with the best view possible.

Base your choice on your personal preferences and on what feels good to you. Know that you are flexible enough to change where you are, if needed. Move closer, farther, or to the side to really experience what you would like to experience.

Make it perfect for you, you deserve it!

That IS happiness!

Day 297

Think of a washing machine!

It takes little breaks and "slow down" moments while in the cycle of washing the clothes. Sometimes it even stops so the laundry can soak before spinning like crazy again. This guarantees a job well done, and it probably would break down or rip clothing if it would spin like crazy for the whole cycle.

Now think of a garbage truck! Once the garbage cans are emptied into it, the truck slows down to digest and work on what it just received. If it would not take that pause it would clog up and stop working.

It is the same for you!

In order to get things done in a healthy and happy way, even if you're tough (like a washing machine or garbage truck), you need to take little breaks and slow down moments for yourself. If not, your "to-do-list" turns into a "have-to-do list". Not a high-for-life frequency at all.

Taking little breaks lets you shift into your now, connect with what is happening right now, and digest all in a healthy and relaxed way.

Breaks are key!

That IS happiness!

Day 298

Imagine that you got all dressed up, and went to a dance.

You said, "I have my dance shoes on. I am ready to dance, frolic, and play." and that's exactly what you did! You danced, frolicked, and played to all kinds of different music. All night long. You were happy, full of energy, joyous, alive, and in your high-for-life frequency.

Life is that magnificent dance, gifting you with the opportunity to get all dressed up! Put on your dance shoes; go dance, frolic, and play to all kinds of adventures it has to offer you.

So, in your new day:

- Let your physical body dance. It is meant to move, to be alive, and to experience all kinds of adventures!
- Let your mind live all that life is offering you. It is designed to experience all of it!
- Let your soul feel your high-for-life energy. It is here to indulge in it all!
- Let consciousness "wow" you in your NOW. It wants you to enjoy it!

Life offers you to BE and live in your high-for-life frequency! So what are you waiting for?

That IS happiness!

Day 299

Do you remember when you encountered sparkles as a child?

You saw, heard, smelled, tasted, thought, and felt them. They were real for you and you believed in them. They shifted you to BE and live in their frequency of magic, *angelic-ness*, light, playfulness, happiness, and being enchanted. Felt great, right?

So go and look out for sparkles again:

- In rain drops touched by sunshine.
- In glimmering lighting in stores.
- Sparkles on clothing and accessories.
- Sparkles on ice, food, and drinks.
- Sparkles on crafting glitter.
- Sparkles in laughing eyes.

Seeing and feeling sparkles makes your inner child light up. It lets you see through your child eyes and feel though your child heart. An enchanting frequency to be in!

In your new day, be a spark, with sparkling your happiness as bright as you can! And enjoy being a *sparkle-ologist*!

That IS happiness!

Day 300

Imagine that you are watching the most beautiful sunset ever!

It is the sun's way of waving at you, saying "This was a magical day. I am going to shut down now. Let's start new tomorrow. See you bright and early!"

Now imagine yourself watching the most beautiful sunrise ever! It is the sun's way of saying "Hello, are you ready to have some fun today? Let's go!"

Take the sun's teaching:

- Start new every morning by greeting and opening up to your new day. Invite all miracles to arrive. Show gratitude for what is for you.
- At night, close your day by thanking and blessing your lived day. Say goodbye by letting go of all not-fitting, and gratefully celebrate all that is fitting for you.

This brings a freshness and a "starting over" energy to every new day you get to live.

You can start over every single day, so relax!

That IS happiness!

Day 301

Being happy is your natural state of being!

When you are happy, your physical health is at its peak. Your mind thinks positive thoughts. Your soul feels good and is heard loud and clear. Your consciousness is vivid. Life is going great for you, good things come your way, and nothing (not even the un-fitting) can shift you from being and living in your high-for-life frequency.

Happiness is always present in you, everything, and everyone. It is never "not" there—you just have to choose to tune in and see, hear, smell, taste, think, and feel it. That will shift you to BE and live in your frequency of happiness.

This joyful feeling comes in different shapes, sizes, and ways; simply breathing, being grateful, kind, helpful, smelling the scent of a cup of tea, meditating, exercising, giving or receiving a smile, spinning your body in circles, lighting a candle, enjoying a glass of wine, shopping, or planning a trip. That is all happiness!

Finding something good in everyone and everything counts as happiness too; cleaning your house and focusing on the good feeling outcome of freshness is happiness.

It is simple; if it makes you feel good, it is happiness and if you mindfully focus on your own happiness - as well as on all the other bits of happiness around you - you simply have to feel good!

That IS happiness!

Day 302

Imagine that this is the story of your new day:

The first thing you feel is a cold draft in your face coming through the window. Then, while getting ready, you hear a bird chirping in your backyard. When you leave your house, the sun blasts you in your face. On your way to work, you see trees. Later that day the rain gets you wet and on your way home the smell of a bakery fills your nose. Finally back home, you drink a glass of water.

Every single one of those happenings is here for YOU!

- The cold draft is here for you to feel.
- The bird is singing for you to hear.
- The sun is shining for you to enjoy.
- The trees are here for you to see and breathe fresh air.
- The rain is here for you to experience.
- The bakery is *fragrancing* the air for you to indulge in the smell.
- The water is here for you to hydrate and taste.

Everything is always here for you to experience. Even the subway screeching in your ear, the angry person on your way to work, and the dust bunny under your couch. They are all here for you, in the same way your birthday cake is there to celebrate you.

So why should you even consider being anything but grateful and excited about what shows up for you and not simply react to everything and everyone like it is your birthday cake, knowing that it is here to celebrate you and your new day?

Say or think "Thank you for showing up and being here for me!" as often as you can. Shift yourself to be and live in the frequency of amazing co-creation with what is here for you.

That IS happiness!

Day 303

Compliments carry the energy of honor, gratitude, appreciation, kindness, and love.

Four fabulous things happen automatically by complimenting yourself, everyone, and everything:

First, you notice something striking that's worth complimenting. In that split second, you are present in your NOW, and that is where your power to choose happiness lays. Plus, you are in awe, which is always an exciting state to be in.

Second, noticing that striking *something* shifts you to BE and live in the high-for-life frequency of that *striking-ness*.

Third, when you compliment someone, you touch their heart. That shifts both - you and that someone - to BE and live in the heart.

Fourth, both of you turn into magic wands. You touch and enchant everyone and everything you encounter with your high-for-life energy.

If you ever feel your magic fading, simply notice something striking and go wild with complimenting yourself, everyone, and everything about it!

One compliment at a time, multiplying goodness with infinite speed and reach!

That IS happiness!

Day 304

Imagine that you are in a wildlife park and even though everyone told you about all the wild animals you'd get to see, you see nothing. So, you walk deeper into the park - but still, nothing.

You decide to have a seat, and give it some time for the animals to show themselves. You quietly sit, and sit, and sit with your eyes wide open. Sure enough, they start to move and show themselves. You are happy you decided to sit and wait. What a magical reward!

Not every treasure and miracle in your life shows itself in a huge and visible way. When you are hurried and in a state of "I want," you can easily miss some of them, but if you pause, sit, go still, and are open to anything, you will see EVERY treasure and miracle that is there for you.

I promise you, you will be happy you sat down, and the reward of experiencing all treasures and miracles will be magical.

That IS happiness!

Day 305

Have an appreciation chat with your physical body! The best time is while drying yourself after a nice warm shower or bath. You'll feel all clean, warm, gentle, soft, and cozy - and your heart will be wide open. So here it goes:

- Massage-dry your head. Say "This is an appreciation massage for you, my superstar head. Thank you for holding it all together!"
- Dry your hair. Say "Thank you for being my luscious asset. I love you."
- Dry your face. Say "I thank you for giving me amazing expressions."
- Dry your neck and shoulders. Say "Thank you for carrying my super-star head so regally."
- Dry your arms and hands. Say "Thank you for being my octopi—making it possible to do lots of things."
- Dry your back and buttocks. Say "Thank you for holding me up and letting me sit down."
- Dry your legs. Say, "Thank you for walking for me and taking me dancing."
- Dry your strong feet. Say "Thank you for carrying me with amazing stamina and elegance."

Make this chat fitting and fun for you! When finished, close your eyes and feel your shift to BE and live in your high-for-life frequency of being healed, healthy, and happy!

That IS happiness!

Day 306

Imagine waking up and seeing, hearing, tasting, smelling, and thinking only about all magic there is; in you, everybody, and everything. Feel the amazing tone you are setting for your new day!

Magic carries the energy of special, abundant, limitless, everything is possible, vivid, alive, and energized. Focusing on all of the magic in and around you shifts you to BE and live in that high-for-life frequency. You fill every single cell of your body, mind, soul, and consciousness with it, and go on sharing this goodness without limits.

So:

- Notice and feel all of the magic in you!
- Notice and feel all of the magic in every breath you take!
- Notice and feel all of the magic in others!
- Notice and feel all of the magic in your food and drinks!
- Notice and feel all of the magic in the air, sounds, and colors!

Magic is always there! Simply tune in, feel and experience it, and multiply it by sharing!

That IS happiness!

Day 307

Stretch your body, mind, soul, and consciousness!

The word "stretch" carries an energy of opening up, being capable of receiving, flowing, health, and flexible. When you stretch, use the word "stretch" or notice all of the stretch in everything and everyone, you shift to BE and live in a stretchy frequency.

Stay loose by stretching your physical body often. A stretched body is a flowing, healthy, and happy body.

Stretch and loosen up your mind by thinking different thoughts, visiting and observing foreign places and cultures, listening to different music and sounds, learning different languages, and tasting different foods. Stretch your mind into *openminded-ness* with something new.

Stretch your soul by letting it help you in every aspect of your physical experience. Have it stretch far to get you the answers you need. A soul always knows.

Stretch your consciousness. Close your eyes. Visualize and feel your consciousness stretch wide, long, and big with every breath you take. Feel it move, from side to side and in waves. Play with it, make it feel good for you, and enjoy your stretched consciousness.

Put on stretchy clothes and shoes. Dance to music to keep you loose and stretched. Surround yourself with stretchy, open-minded people. Play with a stretch band (or silly-putty) and stretch-play all day long, because if you play stretch, you shift to being stretched.

A space of unlimited creative possibilities!

That IS happiness!

Day 308

Imagine that you are at a fork in a road.

Both ways are the same length, and both lead you home. The only difference is that one will have the sun shining brilliantly in your face, and the other offers cool shade.

- Which one will you choose?
- Which one feels better for you?
- Which one do you enjoy more?

In your new day, notice all situations offering you intersections to get you to the same destination. Chose the way that feels better for you over the one that is just routine or comfort. Consciously think this through!

Take charge with your choices and make your days more fitting for you!

The more fitting they are, the happier you can be.

That IS happiness!

Day 309

Shift yourself, everything, everyone, and the world to happiness!

What would happen for you and the whole world if you would write "Be happy!" on sticky notes and place them everywhere, or hand them out with a huge smile?

A shift would happen! A shift for you, everything, everyone, and the whole world to BE and live in a high-for-life frequency of happiness; because everything is energy, connected, and shares its energy. That is how much power you have!

So:

- How many notes (on paper, email, text, or message) of "Be happy!" can you gift others with during your new day?
- How many times can you say "Be happy!" to others?
- How can you inspire others to do the same?

Don't stop there... Where can you see, think, hear, taste, smell, and feel "happiness" in your new day? How can you share it with everyone and everything around you?

Any happiness you create shifts the whole world a little more into a joyous frequency.

Don't hold back, be that happiness creator and initiator!

That IS happiness!

Day 310

Imagine that you are deep cleaning your outside, and inside, while standing under a waterfall.

The water is flowing over your skin, washing everything old and impure away. You feel refreshed and new on the outside!

Now imagine the water entering your being at the top of your head, washing through your insides all the way down, exiting at the bottom of your feet and cleaning out all the old and impure. You feel refreshed and new on the inside.

This imagination shifts you to a frequency of *clean-ness* inside and out, experiencing your new day as fresh and clean. And practicing this cleansing before falling asleep lets everything un-fitting from your day dissolve, and promises you a clean and fresh sleep.

Stay clean! Stay fresh! It's the best feeling ever!

That IS happiness!

Day 311

Being grateful for *something* is a wonderful frequency to be in.

Being what I call "grateful for nothing," however, shifts you to BE and live in an even "higher for life" frequency.

What I mean by nothing is that your gratefulness is not attached to anything else but you simply "being."

So how can you be grateful for nothing?

By sitting in stillness with closed eyes, by focusing on your breath, and by practicing gratitude for simply being.

In your new day, take time to stop being a busy bee. Stop seeing. Stop hearing. Stop speaking. Stop thinking. Stop feeling, Stop smelling. Stop tasting. Stop looking forward or back. Stop wanting anything different, bigger, better, or new. Stop it all! Breathe! Then say or think, "I am grateful for simply being!"

Feel your shift to BE and live in that grateful goodness.

That IS happiness!

Day 312

Imagine that you are taking your heart on a love trip! So let's go!

The first stop is the Eiffel Tower in France. You and your heart are standing on top, looking over beautiful Paris. It is evening. The sunset is breathtaking, and as the dark moves in, the night lights of Paris awaken and enchant you. There is a pulse over the city which carries the energy of love, romance, and beauty. Your heart fills to the brim with this high-for-life energy. Feel this! Time to say goodbye to Paris and welcome your next stop!

Africa! You and your heart join the adventure of a safari. You hop into a jeep and drive though this majestic nature. You see lions, giraffes, and elephants. It is powerful to see them close up. This carries the energy of majestic, powerful, adventurous, and breathtaking. Your heart fills to the brim with this high-for-life energy. Feel this! Time to wave Africa goodbye and welcome your next stop!

Hello Rome! You and your heart hop on a scooter and drive through the warm evening streets. You have dinner outside in a small restaurant. The food is bliss, the scenery romantic, and the wine is joy. After dinner you stumble upon a street festival with music. You dance and flow like never before. This carries the energy of love, bliss, joy, vividness, laughter, movement, and flow. Your heart fills to the brim with this high-for-life energy. Feel this! Time to move to your next spot. You wave Rome goodbye.

You arrive at an island in the Pacific Ocean. You and your heart run to the beach and soak in the beauty of the blue sky, white beach, turquoise water, magical sunshine, and fresh air. This carries the energy of beauty, warmth, *free-ness*, and relaxation. Your heart fills to the brim with this high-for-life energy. Feel this!

By now your heart is overflowing with high-for-life energies, radiating to every single cell of your body, mind, soul, and consciousness - and you are spreading this goodness to everything and everyone around you.

You promise your heart that from now on you let it feel to its highest capacity, and that you keep your heart tank filled with magical feelings at all times. You will let your heart taste like it never tasted before, see like it never seen before, laugh like it never laughed before, enjoy like it never enjoyed before, live like it never lived before and love like it never loved before.

You and your heart, the love story of your life!

That IS happiness!

Day 313

This is a new day! Start fresh, be present, and live simple!

New carries the energy of unused and clean. *Day* carries the energy of living, possibilities, and adventure. *Fresh* carries the energy of pure and clear. *Present* carries the energy of now. And *simple* carries the energy of uncomplicated, effortless, and straight-forward.

When you live your new day as fresh, present, and simple you shift to BE and live in a high-for-life frequency.

To stay fresh and present say or think:

- For today, I accept all that IS.
- For today, I respect all that IS.
- For today, I appreciate all that IS.
- For today, I thank all that IS.
- For today, I love all that IS.
- For today, I choose happiness!

To stay simple, remind yourself of the following:

Yesterday WAS my beautiful yesterday.
Tomorrow will BE my beautiful tomorrow.
Today IS my beautiful new and fresh NOW!

Go and create your best fresh, present, and simplest new play-day ever!

That IS happiness!

Day 314

Imagine you just woke up, and all you can think of, feel, hear, taste, smell, and see is the confidence in you, everyone, and everything. Feel the successful tone that you are setting for your new day!

Confidence carries the energy of strength, *sure-ness*, power, knowing, trust, and being in charge. Focusing on all confidence in and around you shifts you to BE and live in that high-for-life frequency. Go on sharing it with everyone and everything around you.

Acknowledge and feel all confidence in your body; every breath you take, every heartbeat you feel, every muscle being used, and every strength created by your mind, soul, and consciousness. You have a lot of confidence going for you!

Notice all confidence in others, nature, the air, the sky, food and drinks, colors and sounds. Put on confident clothing and shoes, watch a confident movie, or write confident sayings on post-its for you to read. These will all shift you to BE and live as your best confident you!

That IS happiness!

Day 315

Ask yourself "What energy am I in need of right now?"

Find something carrying or acting on the energy you are looking for, feel it, and shift to BE and live in the frequency you are in need of. For example:

- Do you need support? Lean on a wall. Walls are always supportive.
- Do you need flow? Drink water, or play with water. Water is always flowing.
- Do you need coziness? Enjoy a candle light or a bubble bath, both are cozy.
- Do you need softness? Feel a soft blanket.
- Do you need grounding? Walk barefoot. It is always grounding.
- Do you need sweetness? Taste honey, which is pure sweetness.
- Do you need your life spiced up? Indulge in spicy food.
- Do you need clarity? Look at a clear glass, because it knows clarity.

Say you are looking for love. Hold and feel a gift that was given to you with love. Doing so shifts you to BE and live in the frequency of said love. This gift shares its programmed love with you, because everything is energy, connected, and shares its energies.

Play and have some fun with this!

That IS happiness!

Day 316

Imagine that you are looking in the mirror and see a strand of hair in your face.

To fix it, you move the strand out of your face. It would never occur to you to touch the mirror and fix your mirror-self.

All encounters and relationships with other people are your mirrors!

They all show you something! To find out what they mirror in you, ask yourself, "What does this have to do with me? Why does this bother me?" Listen to your inner voice telling you all about it, then fix or heal your feelings in and on you with changes, shifts, and solutions that fit you, and only involve you.

Because fixing anything in or on others is like trying to fix a stray strand of hair on your mirror-self. It won't work!

Don't forget to shower ALL your mirrors with gratitude!

That IS happiness!

Day 317

What state are you the happiest in?

- While being active or inactive?
- While moving or being still?
- While being busy or not busy?
- While being quiet or loud?
- While speaking or being in silence?
- While at home or out and about?
- While alone, with a person, or with lots of people?

Asking this at the beginning of your new day will help you find your sweet spot for where you feel your happiest you. It is a clarity generating tool letting you plan and create a perfect day.

For instance: if today you are at your happiest when you are active, moving, and out and about, plan your new day mostly like that with little pauses here and there to recharge. This guarantees a day of joy for you.

Be at your fullest potential to experience everything that is for you by creating your perfect new day!

That IS happiness!

Day 318

Imagine a mountain!

Strong, unmovable, a bit intimidating, majestic, beautiful, and serious. It carries the energy of: I am always here, you can lean on me, I am in charge, but don't mess with me.

Seeing, hearing, tasting, smelling, thinking, and feeling like a mountain shifts you to BE and live in this strong high-for-life frequency. It's perfect for when life is challenging, because it gives you the strength to pull through for yourself and be strong for others.

Here is a sweet example:

When my husband left for a business trip, our kids were pretty sad he was gone. I told the kids they needed to come and see the mountains that were in clear view. As we peeked at them, I said "See those strong, beautiful, big mountains? That is how strong I am for you right now, so lean on me." This shifted all of us to BE and live in that strong frequency. It was an easy example for the kids to understand the strength I was offering them; and for giggles, one said "Great, because I am the Leaning Tower of Pisa at the moment."

Have an image of a strong mountain handy. Look at it and feel its energy often to gain strength for what is happening for you right now.

In your new day, be a mountain for yourself and others!

That IS happiness!

Day 319

Be the Queen or King you are meant to be! Your throne is ready - yours to sit in - and your kingdom is ready, yours to rule. Actually, it needs you! Close your eyes and visualize yourself arriving as the regal Queen or King you are. Majestically take your seat in your grand throne. Feel your readiness to rule and protect, and your excitement to see all of your magnificent kingdom. In this imagination:

- The Queen or King is your physical body.
- The throne is your soul.
- The ruling is your mind.
- Your kingdom is your consciousness.

Honor your physical you, seat yourself inside your soul, let your intelligent mind rule and protect your truth, and play in your consciousness with excitement. It is all yours, ready for you to take over!

Plus, the words "Queen" and "King" carry the energy of regal, majestic, grand, luxurious, and noble. "Throne" carries the energy of importance, rich, magnificence, and beauty; "ruling" carries the energy of power and being in charge; and the word "kingdom" carries a majestic, empowered, large, strong, and successful energy.

Add all of these energies together, and you've got yourself a potent energetic power house. When you say, feel, think, see, and hear this it shifts you to BE and live in these high-for-life frequencies - and that IS where magic exists! Have fun being a Queen or King!

That IS happiness!

Day 320

Imagine that you are waking up to a fresh new day!

All you can see, hear, taste, smell, and think about is the *alive ness* and life that is in you, everybody, and everything. Feel the vivid tone you are setting for your new day!

"Life" carries the energy of love, light, aliveness, vividness, well-being, abundance, limitless, wonder, and energy. Focusing on all life in and around you shifts you to BE and live in that high-for-life frequency. You fill every single cell of your body, mind, soul, and consciousness with it, and share this goodness with everyone and everything.

This is an easy and always possible task, because life is always present:

- Notice all life in every breath you take.
- Notice all life in your food and drinks.
- Notice all life in the air and the sky.
- Notice all life in colors, sounds, and play.
- Notice all life in every smile and laugh.
- And notice life in you being happy!

Consciously be life, feel life, and live while being vividly alive!

That IS happiness!

Day 321

Close your eyes and visualize water as it shows itself to you. Feel, hear, taste, smell, see, and think of that water. How do you experience this?

Water is the energy of life, the flow, refreshment, coolness, clearness, and hydration. You are mostly made of water, so you ARE already all these amazing energies. Becoming aware of this fact shifts you to BE and live in this wonderful frequency. So does imagining, noticing, and hanging out with water.

Now bless your visualized water with your shiniest smile and your bountiful love. How does it feel now?

Water is very programmable. Being positive and loving towards water adds positiveness and love to its already existing goodness of energy. Blessing water adds the energy of your blessings to it.

So when you bless all water in you with love, you have an unstoppable flowing love-ocean flushing and gushing inside of you. Feel this!

In your new day, be present with - and bless the water - you are about to drink, the rain, the ocean, the shower water, your tears, and any pictures or sounds of water you encounter.

Let loose and become crazy about water!

That IS happiness!

Day 322

Imagine a balcony!

- It lets you step out of wherever you are.
- It lets you look at where you are from the outside.
- It lets you change scenery.
- It presents a quick way to recharge, relax, and enjoy the view.
- It presents a place where you can breathe and rest.
- It presents a place to change the energy of your now.

What balcony can you create in your new day in order to:

- Step out of what is happening for you right now?
- Look at what is happening for you, from the outside?
- Change scenery to something better for you?
- Breathe. Recharge. Relax. Enjoy the view of something better or different?
- Change the energy of what is happening right now?

Your balcony can be a couple hours in a park, sitting in quiet, a trip to the sauna, a vacation, or anything that lets you step out of what is, so you can stop and reflect—before you take action. If you do have a balcony, step out often and consciously embrace the opportunity of the reset this balcony gifts you with. Happy *balcony-ing*!

That IS happiness!

Day 323

You, everything, and everyone have a value!

Everything going great for you has value. Everyone you like and love have value. Those are very easy to acknowledge and live because they feel good and add high-for-life value to your experience. No battle at all.

But so does everything that does not feel good, and everyone you don't like or love. They all have immense value for you and for themselves. Acknowledge their enormous value and focus on that. You will shift from dislike, to liking everything and everyone for the value they are.

With that, you honor and celebrate yourself, everything, and everyone for what it really is.

That IS happiness!

Day 324

Imagine a street sweeper truck with brushes underneath.

It is sweeping and cleaning. While it does that, people with large brooms sweep the trash into piles in front of it (at least that is how they do it in Italy!). They are not there or able to clean for the sweeper truck, but they are there and able to make the trash more visible and help it stay in a straight forward line while it is sweeping and cleaning.

You have the same capability as that street sweeper truck. You are able to clean and sweep all your non-fitting happenings, feelings, and thoughts in your road of life. Everyone you encounter is a person with a broom, sweeping everything into piles into the middle of your life. They are not there or able to do the cleaning for you, but they are there and able to help you see it better while staying focused on your forward journey.

The people you like make piles of joy. No sweeping needed, simply look, smile, and enjoy.

The people you don't like make piles of YOUR non-fitting happenings, feelings, and thoughts. It is yours to see clearly, yours to sweep, and yours to clean.

Happy sweeping!

That IS happiness!

Day 325

"Yay! Everything is under control! I am so happy!"

Sounds great, until you lose that control.

Keeping everything under control is exhausting and against your nature of flowing with this ever-changing physical life. If you do happen to establish some sort of control, once lost, you create a huge amount of un-happiness; and it takes a lot of your energy trying to re-establish it. That is precious energy which could go into feeling happy.

A better way to see, feel, hear, smell, taste, and think is:

"Yay! Everything is as it is. I accept, respect, appreciate, thank, and love everything as it is."

That shifts you to BE and live in peace with how things are right now. A resistance-free frequency, in which you can practice gratitude for what is happening for you. From there, you can think about a new, a different, and a better fitting IS for you.

Nothing is ever under control! Because everything is always simply as it IS!

That IS happiness!

Day 326

Imagine a street musician playing the violin to music coming from a stereo. That was the scenery for one of my walks on a sunny warm day.

On the street side with the musician, people walked in a similar pace. Some smiled, laughed, or had a peaceful lost-in-their-world look. The energy was light, balanced, peaceful, and happy. I felt everything and everyone as connected.

On the other side of the street, nothing and nobody seemed to be fitting with each other, or connected. People walked heavily and with different paces. Some were stressed or angry and only few smiled or laughed. The energy was heavy and unhappy.

That musician - with their music - connected everyone and everything to be ONE. They spread beautiful energy and shifted all - as ONE - to BE and live in a high-for-life frequency.

Be that street musician in your new day! Gift yourself, everything, and everyone with your beautiful energy (it does not have to be through music!). Connect everyone and everything to be ONE, and shift all - as ONE - to BE and live in a high-for-life frequency.

You have that power!

That IS happiness!

Day 327

Think of your eyes as neutral seers giving you a neutral picture to look at and depending on which glasses you choose to wear, you will see, hear, taste, smell, think, and feel differently about your new day. This will decide how your day is going and will be going.

There are many different glasses: happiness and joyous glasses, peaceful and loving glasses, playful and abundant glasses, angry, frustrating, and sad glasses... Just to give you an idea.

Take some time and choose fitting high-for-life glasses through which you want to experience your new day. Choose one pair for your whole day, or practice *openminded-ness* by choosing multiple glasses and switching them often.

Enjoy the view!

That IS happiness!

Day 328

Imagine a fire hydrant.

It always has enough water and is ready to give as much as needed. All it requires to unleash is to be connected to the right hose and someone to open the valve, and here it comes flushing and gushing out into the open.

You are that fire hydrant! You always have enough energy and are ready to give as much as needed. All your energy requires to unleash is that you connect to it and open the valve. And here it comes; flushing and gushing through your body, mind, soul, consciousness, and beyond.

Your personal connection to your energy is achieved by acknowledging, trusting, and believing in your energy. By accepting, respecting, appreciating, thanking, and loving it; and by feeling, seeing, hearing, tasting, smelling, and thinking of your energy!

You open the valve by shifting to BE and live in your high-for-life frequency with practicing anything that makes you happy.

And here it comes, flushing and gushing...

If you like, imagine that you are a fire hydrant, connecting the the hose, opening the valve, and letting your energy flush and gush through you and beyond. That will unleash your beautiful, powerful, and always "happy to serve you" energy.

Let it flow!

That IS happiness!

Day 329

We all look in the mirror every day, quick and fast to get ready! One last look before we leave. Looking good, let's go!

Remember, you are not looking consciously at YOU though. You look in a hurry, without feeling yourself, and most likely while thinking about your new day.

Spending conscious time with yourself in front of the mirror pulls your mind, soul, and consciousness into a tight connected relationship with your physical body. It also creates a deep awareness of your physical body, initiating gentleness and self-love - both of which are essential to experience a happy you.

In your new day, take quiet time to look at yourself in detail. See and feel yourself. Acknowledge all thoughts and feelings coming up without judgment. Say, or think, to every part of your body "I love you!"

Also have some fun... Smile, be angry, sad, or even jealous while looking at yourself. Sing, act, do yoga, or dance while seeing yourself. Eat and drink in front of the mirror.

Get yourself a small pocket mirror to have access to your spectacular looks at all times. And have the most amazing chats while at it. Saying "Hey gorgeous, you look amazing today," while looking at yourself goes a long energetic way.

Take every chance you get and look in those mirrors!

That IS happiness!

Day 330

Imagine yourself at a cafe getting a cup of coffee or tea, paired with a yummy pastry.

You are sending a lot of expectations out there while doing that!

- An expectation that the coffee or tea is of amazing quality, making a yummy cup for you.
- An expectation that the water is the perfect temperature.
- An expectation that the cup is clean.
- An expectation that the milk is fresh, and the amount of sugar is just right.
- An expectation that the pastry is fresh.
- An expectation that this is a high-for-life experience for you.

Expectations and the act of expecting something carry the energy of knowing what you want, and trusting that things will go that way. When you expect you send wishes into consciousness, getting them a chance to be heard and become.

Every split second has lots of possibilities for you to expect. Use all that expecting to your advantage by expecting only the good.

That IS happiness!

Day 331

Take a heart-break!

Love yourself in a big way by breathing yourself into your heart. Use every breath in to open your heart wide and big. Use every breath out to go deeper and deeper inside of your heart. Practice this and see, hear, taste, smell, think, and feel how safe, perfect, healing, and enlightening it is for you to be there.

- You will feel that you don't have to hurry, because there is always enough time for everything.
- You will hear that you don't have to worry, because you are always supported.
- You will see that you don't have to stress, because there is nothing ever important enough to stress about.
- You will realize that you don't have to be negative, because nothing is ever born negative in the first place.
- You will come to understand that you don't have to live the non-fitting happenings, because you can always change them into fitting ones.

There is no need to give hurrying, worrying, stressing, *nega-tive-ing*, and anything un-fitting any of your energy - but every need to give slowing down, trusting, relaxing, *positive-ing*, and the fitting ALL of your energy.

In your new day, celebrate yourself big time and take your heart-breaks often! You deserve it.

That IS happiness!

Day 332

Imagine that it is nighttime and you forgot where you parked your car.

You know for sure it's here. You think it might be in the B lot, but are uncertain. First, you ask yourself, "Where did I park my car?" Then, you tune into yourself, retrace your steps, and try to remember where your car is. Next, you turn on the flashlight to bring light into this darkness and situation, and go find your car.

When your NOW feels dark or uncertain, ask yourself, "Where did I park my happiness?" Tune into your inner you, retrace your steps, and try to remember where you left it and what happiness is for you. Be assured, it's still there! Then, turn on your inner flashlight; your love and light. Shine it bright, and re-find and re-join your happiness.

Shift yourself to BE and live in a high-for-life frequency, no matter what your darkness or uncertainty is about. From there you can practice to accept, respect, appreciate, thank, and love all that is for you. Darkness and uncertainty will shift with you, back into lightness and certainty.

That IS happiness!

Day 333

Stay true to yourself and do all your feel-good doing!

But mindful of how you do it and how everything and everyone around you is impacted by your doing.

Here is the best example ever:

Picture me, writing on my phone, with a kitty on my lap. A wonderful sight, right?

With one exception: I'm frantically and forcefully scrolling down to the bottom of my note. My whole body shakes from side to side. It's nothing bothersome for me, since I am the determined *scroller*, but for my kitty, it means he is shaking too while trying to meditate us both into magic. This is very disruptive for him and he clearly does not like it. Which adds disliking energy to my already frantic and forceful state. Not a very high-for-life energy mix. And because everything is connected we share this mix with each other, everything, and everyone around us.

Noticing this, my swiping got gentle and loving. I stopped shaking, enabling him to be still and happy. That shifted us both to BE and live in a wonderful frequency. Our co-creation together became magic!

In your new day, become aware of what you co-create, and be determined to co-create magic!

That IS happiness!

Day 334

Imagine that you are sitting on a beautiful strong horse!

You are both excited and ready to go on this riding adventure. At first, you keep the reigns short and tight, which means the horse cannot move or go. You and your horse are stuck. Then, you realize if you loosen the reigns, giving them some playroom, the horse can move and go. Which means you both are off to an amazing ride.

The reigns of your life have the same needs: to be loose and have playroom. Your life cannot freely flow and flourish if you hold tight control and keep the reigns short with rules over rules. When you let go, it can rearrange itself for your highest good. Miracles and magic can pop up for you, and experiences that you did not even know existed, can happen for you. You and your life are off to an amazing ride.

Surrender to all that is happening for you.
Accept, respect, appreciate, thank, and love all.
Trust that all is as it supposed to be, and believe
that you are supported and loved by life.

Then send out your dreams, wishes, and desires. Let them go freely, to be arranged fitting for your highest good while you take the stand of letting it all be.

That IS happiness!

Day 335

All is going right!

Your expectations directly impact your experiences. If you expect that all is going - and will go - right for you, your experience will be of that. Likewise, if you expect that all is going - or will go - wrong for you, you will experience that too.

Try this:

Next time when you are in a challenging situation with chaos, instead of shifting to that chaos, shift your expectation to "All is going right for me, everyone and everything!" Think and feel this towards yourself, every person, the chaos, the ground, and the building of where you are at. That shifts yourself and all to BE and live in a frequency of "All is going right!" You will experience that all is going right - even in the midst of all the chaos - and everyone that is open and receiving, will feel it this way too.

While focusing on your expectation of "All is going right," keep the understanding that different people have different expectations, and will - as a result - have different experiences.

Simply keep your "well-expecting" up and running, while having a blast drenching everything and everyone around you in your "All is going right!" magic.

That IS happiness!

Day 336

Imagine that the first thing you do when you wake up is light a candle.

That candle represents your inner light being lit, welcomed, and celebrated anew for your new day. You carry it with you everywhere you go; to make your breakfast in the kitchen, when you get ready in the bathroom, travel to work, be at work, go to lunch, come back home, and then back to bed... until you close your eyes to go to sleep.

A candle carries the energy of festivity, celebration, coziness, romance, love, and relaxation. A light or flame carries the energy of lighting up, being bright and shining, mystery and power.

Imagining or actually carrying a candle representing your inner light, shifts you to BE and live in a sacred frequency, reminding you of its presence all day long.

You are never without your inner light! But some days you have to be reminded of that.

That IS happiness!

Day 337

The stage is prepared for you. Everything is ready to start. All this show needs is your powerful YOU to show up and commit to play and live your new day as alive, awake, and vivid as possible. Are you ready?

- Use your eyes to see everything as alive. Feel what you see!
- Use your ears to hear everything loud and clear. Feel what you hear!
- Use your taste buds to taste everything fully. Feel what you taste!
- Use your nose to smell everything intensely. Feel what you smell!
- Use your skin to touch everything vividly. Feel what you touch!
- Use your thoughts and think highly positive. Feel what you think!
- Use your heart to produce infinite love. Feel that love!
- Use your inner voice to guide you. Feel that guidance!

Really, really, really put your whole YOU into your new day, and feel yourself!

"Glad you showed up!" your new day says with a smile. "Let's do this every day from now on."

This makes for an alive, awake, and vivid show to experience!

That IS happiness!

Day 338

Imagine that you just rinsed the shampoo out of your hair.

Next, you spread the conditioner and find that it is foaming. You grabbed the shampoo bottle again! You laugh (or not) and say, "Stupid me, not paying attention." You rinse, and finally grab the right bottle to condition your hair.

Reflect on what energy you create, fill yourself with, and share with everything and everyone when you say "Stupid me!"

Even when said with a laugh or smile, these words are hurtful and harmful for your body, mind, soul, and consciousness. They shift you to the opposite of feeling self-love.

In your new day, become aware of any hurtful self-talk. Once noticed, change it into something positive. From stupid me to highly intelligent me, from ugly me to beautiful me, from weak me to strong me. Feel that positive self-talk and how it fills every cell of your body, mind, soul, and consciousness. That shifts you to BE and live in your frequency of honoring yourself.

It is of utmost importance to think and talk very highly of yourself!

That IS happiness!

Day 339

Being curious automatically opens you up to receive all possible experiences available for you.

Curiosity carries the energy of wanting to know, to learn, to understand, and to see, feel, hear, taste, smell, and think more about something or someone. Being curious also connects you to your childlike way of feeling in awe, seeing magic, and believing in miracles.

Saying or thinking "I am curious" lets you indulge in a cupcake, made of all the possible "in awe" moments, decorated with the belief that miracles and magic are right around the corner.

Also, notice all curiosity around you: in people, children, nature, music, movies, and as the written word. That shifts you to BE and live in a high-for-life frequency.

Be a curiousness overachiever in your new day!

That IS happiness!

Day 340

Imagine you have that one best friend who always loves you.

They bring out the best in you, are always there for you, believe in you, and make you laugh. You feel like this connection is the best thing that has ever happened to you. Feels great! Right?

You are that best friend for you!

You are capable of all that love for yourself! You possess the power to bring out the best in yourself; you have the understanding to always be there for you; and you know how to be the biggest believer in you!

You ARE the best connection that has ever happened to you!

So take the best friend job for yourself! It lets you meet all your needs so you can BE the best version of YOU.

When filled to the brim with the best of you, you can then accept one or many second-best friends (other people), or be a second-best friend for another person. That is the purest way of enjoying friendship, and a high-for-life frequency to be in.

In your new day, have fun with your best friend that is always with you, and up for a giggle.

That IS happiness!

Day 341

Co-creation!

When you feel good, no matter the *why* or the *what*, you are in perfect alignment with who you are, and co-create with the universe. Keep rocking your aligned co creation! It suits you!

When you don't feel good, no matter the *why* or the *what*, you are not in alignment, you are co-creating with an "out-of-sync" mind-body-spirit-consciousness-YOU, and are excluding the universe.

If so, stop right there! Acknowledge that you don't feel good without getting emotionally entangled or digging into the *why*. Accept, respect, appreciate, thank, and love what is for you. From there, shift to what does feel good by asking, "What would feel good to me right now?' Listen quietly and clearly as your feel-good solution is given to you through feelings, ideas, thoughts, pictures, or little signs. Trust it, and follow these divine directions.

This shifts you back into alignment and co-creating with the universe in no time.

That IS happiness!

Day 342

Imagine that you start your new day by seeing, hearing, tasting, smelling, and thinking only about all of the health there is in you, everyone, and everything. Feel the healthy tone you are setting for your new day!

Health carries the energy of well-being, abundance, being limitless, vivid, alive, happy, and energized.

Focusing on all health in and around you shifts you to BE and live in a frequency of being healthy. You fill every cell of your body, mind, soul, and consciousness with it, and then go on sharing health with everyone and everything.

There is nothing but goodness created by:

- Noticing all health in you.
- Noticing all health in every breath you take.
- Noticing all health in others.
- Noticing all health in your food and drinks.
- Noticing all health in nature, air, and the sky.
- Noticing all health and wellness in colors and sounds.

In your new day, set your focus to only indulge in health, creating an environment where all unhealthiness simply cannot exist. Powerful!

That IS happiness!

Day 343

Pick a memory when you were the happiest ever!

What was it like? What was the occasion? How did you look and feel? What were your thoughts?

Go on a date! You and your beautiful remembrance, talking and thinking vividly about your happiness. Re-feel it! Smile and bathe in this high-for-life feeling of happiest ever. Become and BE that happiness all over again with every cell of your body, mind, soul, and consciousness.

You will come to realize that your "happiest ever" never left. It can't, because your natural state is happiness. You two are one and the same. Just like honey is sweetness. Sweetness never leaves honey. It can't! They are one and the same.

So, not only do you now know that you ARE happiness, but you also understand that you can trust your happiness to always be there for you. Most importantly, you already are an experienced happiness feeler.

All that is left for you to do is tune in, be open, and receive it freely.

Happiness is healthy. A happy you means a healthy body, mind, soul, and consciousness!

That IS happiness!

Day 344

Imagine that you are enjoying a brand-new, fresh home cooked meal. Once devoured, you put your dirty plate on the counter until it is time for your next meal. You then take the old crusty plate and put the new fresh food on it. Time to enjoy!

The brand-new food will not taste brand-new or fresh with the old food underneath. Not only is the old food not fit for consumption anymore, it was also full of different tastes. Making the experience of the brand-new food impure.

Today is your brand-new day with fresh experiences, but it might not feel brand-new because it is lived through your old experiences; loaded with thoughts, feelings, and beliefs that are like that old food—not fit for consumption anymore. So acknowledge every new day as a clean new plate which you then fill with fresh experiences.

- Feel every breath you take as brand-new. You have never taken this exact breath before.
- Enjoy your coffee and breakfast as brand-new. You have never tasted those exact ones before.
- Live your work day as brand-new. You have not had this work day before.
- Feel your hugs and kisses as brand-new. You never had that exact hug or kiss before.
- Experience your interactions with others as brand-new. Because they ARE new, for you and for them.

Enjoy all this brand-new freshness that is waiting for you!

That IS happiness!

Day 345

Don't get distracted!

We all have valuable plans, lists, and timelines to stay organized - and on track - with our goals in our new day and that is great. But let's be honest; most of the time these plans, lists, and timelines are not the way the day unfolds. Which sets us up for "not feeling good."

Instead, set your focus on only one goal; To BE happy!

Be happy while living your new day in the possible and hopeful ways of your valuable lists, plans, and timelines; but under no circumstances do you get distracted from that one and only goal of being happy.

This guarantees that you feel good, regardless of the expected or unexpected happenings. Your day depends solely on your choice to BE happy, and you will handle everything planned and unplanned in the best way for you—your happy way. I promise that you will succeed every single day that way.

That IS happiness!

Day 346

Imagine a dangling carrot in front of you.

You want it so badly that you chase it. Sadly, you have not caught it by now and even though you are exhausted, you are still focused on running after it which means that you are missing anything else there is for you.

Versus...

A carrot is dangling in front of you. You pause and acknowledge it. You feel it. You realize you want it. You accept, respect, appreciate, thank, and love it. You decide to let it to come to you, and you act and live as it is already yours.

The latter example moves you into your heart. There, you have no need to run *exhaustedly* after anything in your life or miss what's there for you. You can simply see, feel, hear, smell, taste, and think how much you want it, how fitting it is for you, and act on making it happen in a feel-good way. That shifts you to BE and live in your high-for-life frequency, where your heart's desire can come to you as a manifestation.

If, by any chance, it never comes, understand that it was not meant for you. Something better and more fitting for you will show up. The universe will make sure.

There is one exception: if running after your carrot feels good, energizes you, and is a blast, keep running to catch it. It is meant for you to get it in that way. But the moment your good-feeling is gone or exhaustion sets in, pause, and move into your heart to let it come to you.

That IS happiness!

Day 347

You are created. You create. Everything is created.

Your body creates heat, your cells create renewal, and your heart creates love. You create your delicious morning drink, create at work, and create a cozy mood with lighting a candle. You create without ever going on a creation-break! So does everyone and everything else. Life is an ever-going creation.

Consciously acknowledge:

- All creations that are already complete. For instance, this book has already been created for you.
- All in the processes of creation. What you are working on? Are you creating anything breathtaking?
- All the others around you that are creating. What are they creating?
- All the creation in Nature. What is it creating today?

Realizing all creation in and around you, shifts you to BE and live in an inspired frequency, where you can find your power, strength, and infinite boldness to go for what you want to create in your life.

Be the magnificent creator you really are!

That IS happiness!

Day 348

Imagine you decide to see, hear, taste, smell, and think about all of the abundance there is in you, everyone, and everything. Feel the abundant tone you are setting for your new day!

Abundance carries the energy of plentiful, enough, taken care of, beautiful, rich, and full. Focusing on all abundance in and around you shifts you to BE and live in that high-for-life frequency. You fill every single cell of your body, mind, soul, and consciousness with it, and go on sharing this goodness with everyone and everything around you.

Be an abundance spreader through:

- Feeling all abundance in every breath you take.
- Celebrating all abundance within yourself.
- Mentioning all abundance in others.
- Tasting and smelling all abundance in your food and drinks.
- Breathing all abundance in the air.
- Enjoying all abundance in colors, sounds, and music.

Live your new day as an abundant being experiencing an abundant adventure.

That IS happiness!

Day 349

Do it for YOU!

Whatever you are doing right now or are about to do, consciously commit to do it for YOU. That insures that all your doings are of a positive nature, enriching you and your experience of life. Plus, you are in charge that way and run the show for yourself!

Some doings will be easy: like eating some delicious chocolate. You can effortlessly think, see, hear, taste, smell, and feel that you are enjoying this treat for you. You got this one!

Others, like waiting in a long line for a safety-emission test on your car, will need some conscious commitment to think, see, hear, taste, smell, and feel you are doing this for you. In those cases, acknowledge and focus on the part that is for you. As an example: at the emission test, focus on your car being checked for safety. You can easily feel that this part of the doing is for you, because it keeps you safe.

Practicing the "Doing this for YOU" approach lets you realize that every "doing" has a part for you in it.

That IS happiness!

Day 350

Imagine that you are expecting to watch an action movie, but, the movie has no action in it.

First off, it would not count as an action movie. It would not entertain or give you the experience of an action movie. Actually, it would feel boring without the exciting tension. The action makes the movie an action movie.

Now, imagine you expect to live your life, but your life has no conflicts in it. First off, it would not count as life. It would not entertain or give you the experience of life. Actually, it would be rather boring and feel like something is missing. Conflicts make life complete, just as happiness does.

Conflicts are your invitation to grow into your authentic self. They help you figure out what does and does not feel good for you. They bring you closer to who you really are.

In your new day, welcome your conflicts and be entertained by the action they bring for you.

That IS happiness!

Day 351

Imagine that you are listening to a loved one telling you all about their day.

Why would you take your time to do that? Well, because you accept, respect, appreciate, thank, and love them. You are interested in their story and well-being. So you listen and focus while being fully present.

Now imagine your inner voice is talking to you, and telling you all about your day. Do you focus on listening the same way you listen to your loved one?

Your inner voice is an intelligent part of you. It has all the understanding, wisdom, knowledge, and answers you will ever need to truly live your life to the fullest. It deserves your undivided attention!

So become still and invite your inner voice to speak loud and clear. Then, focus and listen. Accept, respect, appreciate, thank, and love what it has to say. I promise you that you will find it interesting, because it is about your story and your well-being.

That IS happiness!

Day 352

Pick your costume!

Have you ever put on a costume and felt different than your usual you? Costumes carry energy, and dressing up in them shifts you BE and live in that certain energy. Use that to your advantage!

Ask yourself "What or who do I want to be in my new day?

If you can, go and dress up in your chosen costume. Have a long look in the mirror and feel your shift. If not, imagine yourself dressing up and feel the shift in energy initiated by this.

For example: If you are a pirate, feel that pirate power. If you are an angel, feel that angelic power. If you are a queen, feel the *regal-ness*. If you are a ballerina, feel the graciousness. If you are a superhero, feel the superhero power. This shifts you to BE and live in the high-for-life frequency of your costume.

Have some fun with this, and certainly share this with your kids!

That IS happiness!

Day 353

Have you ever searched for THE magic in your life?

You being present with your feelings in your NOW is THE magic of your life. And since you are in charge of how and what you feel, you are capable of creating the biggest and best magic you wish to experience.

So:

- Consciously take a deep breath! Feel, hear, smell, taste, see, and think about its life.
- Consciously take a bite of deliciousness! Taste, smell, hear, see, think, and feel its *delectability*.
- Consciously look at something beautiful! See, feel, hear, smell, taste, and think of its beauty.
- Consciously listen to music you like! Hear, feel, smell, taste, see, and think of its power.
- Consciously smell something pleasantly aromatic! Smell, taste, feel, hear, see, and think of its pleasantness.
- Consciously touch your skin! Feel, smell, taste, hear, see, and think about its smoothness.
- Consciously feel, hear, see, taste, smell, and think of your aliveness, brilliance, and ever-moving and vibrating energy.

I say, you can call your search off. Because THE magic of your life is always happening right here and now in YOU.

That IS happiness!

Day 354

Imagine that you are a beautiful songbird.

You are living the life, flying high, eating all the yummy things you can find, and singing the world into a high-for-life frequency. Life is amazing! Until... you see a peregrine falcon waiting for its lunch. What do you do?

Do you quietly find shelter until it moves on? If so, are you going to feel weak and cowardly about yourself?

Or are you flying right into its face? Are you waving at it and taking part in a happening that might not even be yours to take part in? If so, are you going to feel strong and powerful about yourself?

That peregrine falcon represents every non-fitting person you encounter.

Is it really worth it, strong, and powerful if you leave your high-for-life frequency to feed the beast? Or is the most powerful thing to stay in your happiness and maybe share that with them?

I sincerely hope you agree to the latter. But beware! If sharing your happiness is not an option (because the beast is too big or not able to receive) then find shelter in your happiness, and wait until the beast has moved on or shifted to a better frequency.

That IS happiness!

Day 355

Enchantment at its best!

Some of my days take me driving by a house that looks just like the castle of Beauty and the Beast. A fairy-tale place; magical beyond words. I like to think that the people who built this house must believe in fairy tales, miracles, and magic.... And their enchanted ways of living.

This house naturally carries the energy of fairy tales, miracles, magic, and enchantment. Whoever lives there or close by - and whoever notices it - can choose to shift to BE and live in that high-for-life frequency. I certainly do. Then, I continue on my fairy-tale day. And no matter what is happening for me that day I will see, hear, taste, smell, think, and feel everything and everyone through a blanket of enchantment.

Find your "fairy-tale-miracle-magic" shift initiator in your new day. Be aware of it! Choose to shift to its frequency with every cell of your body, mind, soul, and consciousness.

Enjoy your enchanted day!

That IS happiness!

Day 356

When in doubt choose happiness!

Happiness carries the energy of joy, health, abundance, success, vividness, and life. Choosing and creating your happiness means that you are choosing YOU, are creating for YOU, and shift to BE and live in your high-for-life frequency. That goodness fills every cell of your body, mind, soul, and consciousness. Share it with everything and everyone around you.

So:

- When you don't know what to do, choose something that makes you happy.
- When you don't know what to feel, choose feelings of good nature.
- When you don't know what to eat, choose food that makes you feel healthy.
- When you don't know what to wear, choose what makes you joyous.

You will NEVER go wrong with choosing to BE and live happy!

I suggest you tell anything un-happy that you don't have the time to hang out or dig deep into the why. Because, let's face it, you are simply too busy having fun with your happiness. And, by golly, do you enjoy it!

That IS happiness!

Day 357

You are a persistent winner! Win, winning, and winner carry the energy of abundance, happiness, joy, success, vividness, and magnificence. Realizing and saying, thinking, hearing, tasting, smelling, and feeling yourself as a winner shifts you to BE and live in a high-for-life frequency. Here is why I know you are a winner:

- You win every morning by opening your eyes, because you are gifted with another new day.
- You win by stepping out of bed. Because your feet say "I got you, let's go!"
- You win by tasting the first sip of your hot beverage.
- You win by ripping your door open, by stepping out like a wild one, and smelling the world.
- You win by sticking your face into the sunlight, dancing and refreshing in the rain, being picked up for a twirl by strong winds, quieting down with fog, or being enchanted by a winter-wonderland.

You win all life long! Plus, you have the power to create winner moments for yourself and others at any given time— make a spectacular cup of tea, wear clothing that shift you to your "Rocky Balboa" feel, or listen to powerful music. But the most beautiful winner moment is when you inspire others to see the winner in themselves. It shifts them to BE and live in their winning energy, which they will share with you, everything, and everyone around them. Your miraculous stage to create your winning life is ready. What are you waiting for? Go win!

That IS happiness!

Day 358

Pretend that you are an inspector looking for clues and information!

What is it that you are searching for?

Proof of what is needed to make yourself feel the best and most amazing about yourself. And ways in how to make that happen. So:

- You interrogate; to find out what you need to know to feel the best ever about yourself.
- You look through the looking glass; to find the details of what you need to see to feel superb about yourself.
- You ask your inner guidance; to examine the what and the how.
- Then you act on your findings and make it happen.

In your new day, leave no stone unturned to find the clues to feel the best ever about yourself. And feel free to lead the way by doing the same for others.

That makes for a fantastic detective adventure!

That IS happiness!

Day 359

Go inward to BE and relax!

Close your eyes (or leave them open, looking at the sky) and focus on your breath. Breathe deeply. Feel the resetting rhythm of your breathing.

When ready, turn your senses inward:

- Turn all your feeling towards the inside of you and feel yourself inside.
- Turn your eyes towards the inside of you and look at your heart.
- Turn your ears towards the inside of you and hear what is there.
- Turn your instinct towards the inside of you and receive all messages.
- Turn your thoughts towards the inside of you and make them about you.

Turn, BE, and live completely and fully inside of you while making everything NOT inside of you *none of your business*.

Create this conscious inward moment with your breathing often in your new day, and enjoy all the wonderful knowledge and wisdom coming your way!

That IS happiness!

Day 360

Imagine a leaf blowing in the wind!

There are two energies happening here. There is the leaf being blown around: playful, not in charge, and having a bunch of spontaneous fun. And then there is the wind: absolutely in charge, carrying responsibility, and creating all the power and strength for this happening.

In all situations, become aware of what the leaf is and what the wind is. Then, ask yourself "Which energy feels better, being blown around or doing the blowing around?" This gives you clarity for how and what you need to do in order to experience your happening in a fitting energy.

For example: Do you want to be in charge at work, or would you rather be the one going with the flow? Do you want to take charge and make dinner or do you rather want to simply enjoy it? Do you want to be the one organizing your vacation, or rather, would you want to leave that to someone else?

There is always a leaf and a wind energy present, and naturally, your needs change every minute. So, ask often and be conscious about what will it be... the leaf or the wind? Then make it fitting for you.

That IS happiness!

Day 361

Imagine that you have a little glass lantern with a candle inside of your heart.

You open the lantern and take the candle into your hands. You see, hear, taste, smell, think, and feel that candle. You come to understand that this is YOUR candle—YOUR light.

With excitement, you take a match and light it. It is beautiful! You smile and welcome it. You spend some time together.

When ready, you place your light back into the lantern in your heart. You fold your hands by your heart and bow to your light. You feel your bright light lighting up your whole being and shining towards everything and everyone on your outside. Breathe and feel this!

In your new day, feel your bright light lighting you up, and consciously set the intention to shine it onto everything and everyone you encounter. That shifts you, and everything and everyone to BE and live in a high-for-life frequency.

Shine, go shine!

That IS happiness!

Day 362

Be and live like a tree!

- Have strong roots (soul) that ground you.
- Have a strong trunk (physical body) that steadies you.
- Be playful in your crown (mind) to experience happiness.
- Adapt to all happenings (your now) and stay in the flow.
- Communicate (advocate for yourself) with others.
- Share your nourishment (light and love) and accept nourishment if you are in need.
- Bloom (inspirations) when it is time to bloom.
- Let go (un-fitting) when you need to let go.
- Rest (BE) when it is time to rest.
- Heal and grow when you need to heal and grow.
- Be social, but stay pure and true to yourself.

Do it like a tree, adjust and BE.

That IS happiness!

Day 363

Imagine that you are in front of a candy store!

- Are you going to enter or simply keep walking?
- Are you going to stand outside and look at all the candies through the window? Is that enough for you?
- Are you going to enter, buy the first candy at the entrance, and then leave?
- Or are you going to enter, wander around in awe, and take your time to find the candy that makes you feel the happiest?

Now imagine you are in front of your high-for-life experience store!

- Are you going to enter or simply keep walking the comfort path you are already walking on?
- Are you going to stand outside and look at all the possibilities through the window? Is that enough for you?
- Are you going to enter and choose the first one right at the entrance, and then leave?
- Or are you going to enter, wander around in awe, and take your time choosing the high-for-life experience that makes you feel the happiest?

Every new day is that high-for-life experience store!

I cannot tell you enough how important it is for you to be choosy about how and what you want to experience—because everything is always there.

Your responsibility is to choose, and only choose the best for you!

That IS happiness!

Day 364

You don't ever need a reason to breathe. You are your breath! It is automatic and always happening for you.

It is the same for feeling good!

You will never need a reason to be happy, healthy, peaceful, abundant, strong, beautiful, or successful, and you will never need a reason to BE and live in your high-for-life frequency. You already are all of these feelings. They are automatically there and happening for you whenever you want them.

Simply tune in, open up, receive, feel, and live them.

- To tune in: become still and feel your being.
- To open up: feel your breath and your readiness to receive.
- To receive: trust that you are deserving of all this goodness.
- To feel: acknowledge, accept, respect, appreciate, thank, and love all experiences.
- To live them: believe that it is who you really are. A being of goodness!

Kick those silly reasons to the curb!

That IS happiness!

Day 365

Congratulations! You made it! Acknowledge how far you have come in your passion to BE and live in your high-for-life frequency of happiness. See, hear, taste, smell, think, and feel the huge shift you created by showing up every day, reading, and acting on what you were given to understand, love, and cherish about yourself and your life. Consciously admire all of the joy that you created for yourself and shared with everything and everyone around you, and be proud of how much better of a world you built for yourself, everything, and everyone.

I applaud you, and hope you celebrate yourself with the highest regard for becoming a happier person. And I trust you'll keep growing in your job as Happiness Ambassador for All. Go let the corks pop and make it a magnificent bash to celebrate yourself!

That IS happiness!

* * *

Ready for more happiness? Get the companion to this book, the *365 Days of Happiness* journal workbook.

I truly hope you enjoyed *365 Days of Happiness* as much as I loved writing it—please take a short minute to leave a review on Amazon.com and Goodreads.com. Your kind feedback helps other readers find my books easier, and get happier faster. Thank you, you mean the whole cupcake to me! Jacqueline

Also by Jacqueline Pirtle

365 Days of Happiness - Journal Workbook

This enlightening journal workbook is your daily tool to create a habit of living your every day bliss, and is the companion to *365 Days of Happiness: Because happiness is a piece of cake*.

* * *

Life IS Beautiful - Here's to New Beginnings

If you like digging deeper into the meaning of life and are inspired by spirituality, then you'll love Jacqueline's effective teachings.

* * *

Parenting Through the Eyes of Lollipops

A Guide to Conscious Parenting

If you like harmony at home and laughter in the house, then you'll love Jacqueline's inspirational methods.

* * *

What it Means to BE a Woman

And Yes! Women do Poop!

If you like to live free, empowered, and want to decide for yourself, then you'll love Jacqueline's liberating ways.

Want to continue your daily happiness quest?

Here is a peak into my book *Life IS Beautiful*:

BEAUTY AND BEAUTIFUL

Beauty and beautiful is always whatever you want it to be!

The range of what beauty and beautiful means is yours to choose, and can go anywhere from vacationing at the most beautiful place on earth, to wearing the most beautiful outfit ever; or being over the moon about a clean toilet, since it is sheer beauty to sit your bottom onto something that is so squeaky clean.

You are in total charge of your personal relationship to beauty and beautiful!

As we covered in the chapter ***Nothing is Ever Set in Stone***, everything and everyone is energy first and foremost— so are words, feelings, opinions, expectations, and happenings. Everything!

As words, beauty and beautiful carry the energy of special, happiness, bliss, health, nature, betterment, positivity, luxury, glamour, easiness, abundance, wonderful to the eye and heart, a sort of supposed to be like that and naturally as is—and all else that you make it to be.

Seeing, hearing, tasting, smelling, and thinking of - plus feeling - beauty and beautiful is a pure alignment with the untouched natural energetic and physical world, and what it has to offer. This is the natural way of things, until humans strip it away with their actions, ways, and disalignment—then declaring it to be the opposite, ugliness.

Just think of nature and its bountiful wonders. There is nothing but beauty present—even when animals are hunting other animals, the natural beauty of a nourishing value and pure survival is printed in this happening.

This makes for a great case to recondition and align yourself towards beauty all the time, since beauty and beautiful is always there. To think that beauty exists, to hear beauty everywhere, to see the beauty in all, to taste and smell beautifully often, and to feel that beauty is always present in, on, and around you is a powerful clarity—because beauty is inevitable. So why not save your precious energy of the human-proving-it-wrong action to uglify life and instead trust that fact, knowing, and delicious feeling fully and vividly?

Beauty and beautiful is unavoidable and in order to escape it you have to put an enormous effort into dodging and not experiencing it. That effort is exhausting and creates sadness, anger, frustration, and an unlimited amount of unwell-feelings. You might even feel that life is nothing like you want it to be, that none of your desires and wishes are reachable, let alone coming into realization. It's a dilemma that keeps feeding itself by focusing on a reality in which the existence of beauty is denied.

To continue this chapter, buy **Life IS Beautiful** to start living fully today!

About the Author

Bestselling author, podcaster, and holistic practitioner, Jacqueline Pirtle, has twenty-four years of experience helping thousands of clients discover their own happiness. Jacqueline is the owner of **FreakyHealer** and has shared her solid teachings through her podcast **The Daily Freak**, sessions, workshops, presentations, and books with clients all over the world. She holds international degrees in holistic health and natural living. Her effective healing work has been featured in print and online magazines, podcasts, radio shows, on TV, and in the documentary *The Overly Emotional Child by Learning Success*, available on amazon prime.

For any questions you might have, to sign up for Jacqueline's newsletter, and for more information or whatever else she is up to, visit www.freakyhealer.com and her social media accounts @freakyhealer.

Made in United States
North Haven, CT
07 August 2024

55772384R00220